M000191660

Washington 23 September 1999
Mr. Jan Kozielewski
15 Ogrodowa Street
91-065 Lodz

My friend...

After all these years, I can now write to you again at an address in Lodz.
I never imagined this would happen...

You have gone back, back to where you came from.

To the city of your happy and crazy youth.

What has been happening to you, man, since that day in August
1931, when you got on the train at Lodz Fabryczna station? Where
did it take you?

I had no desire for Warsaw,
When I was leaving Lodz.
Rotten twilight glided across the fields,
The train dragged itself like a funeral through the fog

Warsaw, Vilnius, Lvov, Krakow... Paris, London, Washington, New
York, Caracas, Washington...
Tuwim was right, wasn't he?
I'm going to see you. The address I'm writing to is to be valid from
1 October 1999. Maybe, the letter will come in time?
Perhaps we will recognize each other after all these years?
                    Yours (?)

—Letter Jan Karski wrote to himself and sent to the address
of the Museum of the City of Łódź

REMEMBER THIS

THE LESSON OF JAN KARSKI

A PLAY BY CLARK YOUNG AND DEREK GOLDMAN

GEORGETOWN UNIVERSITY PRESS / WASHINGTON, DC

The publisher is not responsible for third-party websites or their content. URL links were active at time of publication.

Library of Congress Cataloging-in-Publication Data

Names: Young, Clark, author. | Goldman, Derek, author.
Title: Remember this : the lesson of Jan Karski / Clark Young and Derek Goldman.
Description: Washington, DC : Georgetown University Press, 2021. | Includes
  bibliographical references.
Identifiers: LCCN 2021011326 | ISBN 9781647121686 (paperback) |
  ISBN 9781647121693 (ebook)
Subjects: LCSH: Karski, Jan, 1914-2000—Drama. | Righteous Gentiles in the
  Holocaust—Poland—Drama.
Classification: LCC PS3557.O3668 R46 2021 | DDC 812/.54—dc23
LC record available at https://lccn.loc.gov/2021011326

∞ This paper meets the requirements of ANSI/NISO Z39.48-1992 (Permanence of Paper).

22 21   9 8 7 6 5 4 3 2   First printing

Printed in the United States of America

Remember This: The Lesson of Jan Karski was originally produced by The Laboratory for Global Performance and Politics at Georgetown University, Derek Goldman and Cynthia Schneider, co-director. The play was adapted into the film *Remember This*, directed by Jeff Hutchens and Derek Goldman, produced by Eva Anisko.

Cover design by Spencer Fuller, Faceout Studio
Interior design by BookComp, Inc.
Epigraph image © Carol Harrison
Film stills courtesy of the film REMEMBER THIS © Sobremesa Media LLC

CONTENTS

FOREWORD

Samantha Power

I first learned of Jan Karski when I watched the epic Claude Lanzmann documentary *Shoah*. He appeared in the film for just forty
minutes out of the nine and a half hours, but the impression he left
was indelible.

Looking back at Professor Karski's life, it is tempting to believe
that he was part of some almost separate species, given his intellectual, moral, and physical courage. But to view Karski this way
actually diminishes what he offers each of us.

Karski was in fact very human.

By his own testimony, he loved to have fun. He surrounded
himself, as a young man, with fast horses and many friends. Aside
from a prodigious memory and facility with a number of languages, he seemed, at an early stage, unexceptional. He had mod-
erate ambitions.

Like many in his generation, he was surprised and horrified
by the war. As a Catholic, he could have survived the occupation,
perhaps, by keeping his head down. But he was genuinely shocked
by Nazi brutality and so infuriated by the aggression against his
beloved Poland that he felt a duty to resist.

His wartime role was primarily that of a courier, a job with a
short life expectancy, demanding the ability, as he put it, "to melt
into the landscape, to seem humdrum and ordinary."[1] Resistance
work also required a deep reserve of guts. Karski's own sister turned

away from him, and many of his colleagues lost their nerve—but Karski just grew ever more committed.

In retrospect, the most amazing feature of this exceedingly dark period is that good people, like Karski, didn't succumb to the despair that must have been very, very tempting. Not only was their homeland of Poland occupied by Hitler's forces on one side and Stalin's on the other, but the swastika held sway virtually everywhere in continental Europe. And without the benefit of hindsight, one can imagine how all-encompassing the doom must have felt. The future must have seemed very clear: freedom had been murdered; liberty was dead.

But humans, thankfully, do not always bow before the facts; we are not simply logical creatures. Karski took on his most famous assignment at the moment of maximum darkness. In the summer of 1942 he was asked to report on conditions inside Poland, to relay messages from various Polish political factions to their counterparts in exile, and to travel with the truth to London.

It's hard to remember from the perspective of today, but it was highly unlikely at that time that the truth would matter. The Holocaust was already under way. Around the town of Chełmno, mobile vans were gassing an average of one thousand people a day. Jews and others in Poland had tried to get the word out, but the first reports were judged too fantastic to be believed. Publishers of newspapers right there in the town, and others, argued that the proof was insufficient, while governments, including that of the United States, shielded themselves from inconvenient knowledge. Walter Lacquer wrote later of the contradictory feeling—and immense denial—that prevailed, observing: "It is, in fact, quite likely that while many Germans thought that the Jews were no longer alive, they did not necessarily believe that they were dead."[2]

The Polish Underground did not ask Karski to include an account of what was happening to the Jewish people in Poland, but Karski was a thorough man. Friends smuggled him through a tunnel and into the Warsaw Ghetto. Disguised as a Ukrainian prison guard, he then infiltrated a transit camp where he witnessed what no outsider was supposed to see: Jews beaten and shot at for sport, then packed into trains.

The images of the sick machinery of the Holocaust were seared into his brain, but Karski knew that the burden of proof would be heavy. So he carried hundreds of documents on microfilm concealed in the shaft of a key, and made a death-defying journey across Nazi Germany, occupied France, and Fascist Spain to the office of the British Foreign Secretary, where he provided one of the first public testimonies of the most depraved singular crime against humanity ever committed. He made the inconceivable undeniable. He punctured the consciousness of those who were prepared to listen.

Unfortunately, most weren't.

He traveled on to the United States, where he met secretly with President Franklin Roosevelt in the summer of 1943 and warned him that the Jews of Poland would soon "cease to exist."[3] Karski would later downplay the impact of this meeting. Roosevelt, however, issued an executive order in early 1944 establishing the War Refugee Board to rescue and resettle persecuted Jews, an effort that ultimately saved tens of thousands of lives. John Pehle, the man in charge of the board, insisted that Roosevelt never would have undertaken such an initiative had it not been for his interaction with Karski. The information Karski brought to Roosevelt, according to Pehle, "changed US policy overnight from indifference to affirmative action."[4]

Karski was a hero. His memory will remain with us. And his legacy of thoroughness and bravery will be sustained. But what does it add up to? What does Karski mean for us today?

During World War II Hungarian writer Arthur Koestler cited the frustration felt by those who first raised the alarm about Nazi atrocities. He observed that those who warned were often only able to reach people for a moment, and then they saw their listeners shake themselves, as he put it, "like puppies who have got their fur wet," and return to the blissful place of uninvolvement. "You can convince them for an hour," Koestler wrote, but then "their mental self-defense begins to work and in a week the shrug of incredulity has returned like a reflex temporarily weakened by a shock."[5]

Koestler wrote more than seven decades ago, so surely we have learned our lesson by now. But when the Burmese military attempts to eradicate the Rohingya people of Myanmar; when the Chinese government locks up over a million Muslim Uighurs in prison camps across Xinjiang; when white supremacists march on an American city chanting "Jews will not replace us"; and when Holocaust denial is enjoying a resurgence, we are reminded that every day each of us has a duty to bear witness, to seek accountability, to pursue justice, and to act in the spirit of Jan Karski.

Karski must have seemed completely naïve at the time—to believe that the facts could make a difference. But he has become a giant of history we wish to resemble. A simple person with straightforward goals: find and tell the truth, and do everything within one's power to ensure that people are not targeted for who they are, what they believe, or to whom they pray.

That is why we must remind ourselves over and over again to be vigilant. And it is why the story of Jan Karski must continue to be told to new generations, reminding them that the courage and ability to act on behalf of vulnerable people is not reserved for a select few—it resides within each of us.

Notes

1. Jan Karski, *Story of a Secret State: My Report to the World* (Washington, DC: Georgetown University Press, 2014), 260.

2. Walter Lacquer, *The Terrible Secret: Suppression of the Truth about Hitler's "Final Solution"* (New York: Penguin, 1982), 201.

3. Quoted in Ed Vulliamy, "Revealer of Holocaust Secret Dies," *Guardian*, July 15, 2000, https://www.theguardian.com/world/2000/jul/16/edvulliamy.theobserver.

4. Quoted in Michael T. Kaufman, "Jan Karski Dies at 86; Warned West about Holocaust," *New York Times*, July 15, 2000, https://www.nytimes.com/2000/07/15/world/jan-karski-dies-at-86-warned-west-about-holocaust.html.

5. Arthur Koestler, "The Nightmare That Is a Reality," *New York Times*, January 9, 1944.

REMEMBER THIS

THE SIMPLE TEACHING OF "AN INSIGNIFICANT MAN"

Madeleine Albright

In the summer of 1942, in occupied Poland, leaders of the patriotic resistance gathered for the purpose of sharing a story with the outside world. Their goal: to present a true account of the terrible persecution wrought by Nazi oppressors against the Polish people. Although the officials quarreled about exactly what to say, there was no doubt who they would ask to carry their report through enemy lines. When the meeting adjourned, they transmitted a clandestine radio message to London: "Karski coming soon. Goes through Germany, Belgium, France, Spain. Inform all 'transfer cells' in France, also all Allied representatives in Spain."[1] Jan Karski's historic journey to the British capital and then onward to the United States provides a climax to Clark Young and Derek Goldman's remarkable one-person play, *Remember This*. The saga it recounts is very much of its own era, but the issues and choices it compels us to confront speak to every generation and most urgently to ours.

The background is this. In the summer of 1939, a twenty-five-year-old Polish diplomat, Jan Karski, was summoned to military service as part of his homeland's mobilization against the threat posed by Nazi Germany. A century and a half earlier, Poland had been overrun by its neighbors, chopped up, and erased from the map. Not until 1918, after World War I, was it reconstituted. During the next two decades, the country labored to prosper despite economic setbacks, political infighting, and the rise of ruthless dictators across its borders to the east and west. In August 1939 German chancellor Adolf Hitler and Soviet premier Joseph Stalin secretly agreed on a plan to invade Poland from two directions. Polish leaders were confident that their efforts at preparedness, bolstered by a newly forged alliance with the West, would keep their nation safe. They were wrong.

Launched on September 1, the two-pronged enemy invasion sliced through Poland and its antiquated armed forces with devastating speed. After a desperate retreat to the east, Karski and the surviving members of his unit were captured by Soviet troops and sent to a forced labor camp. Convinced that other Polish soldiers were still fighting, Karski saw it as his duty to join them. Seizing the opportunity of a prisoner transport, he helped to organize a daring escape during which inmates propelled their comrades—including Karski—through the open windows of a moving train. He then made his way on foot to the capital city, Warsaw, where he swore allegiance to the Polish Underground. This was a hastily organized network of spies, saboteurs, and propagandists who were fighting back against German efforts to destroy Poland's identity and culture.

Jan Karski was a well-liked, well-educated man. Until his mobilization, he had enjoyed an agreeable life and career, serving in the military and in diplomatic positions in Germany, Switzerland, and Great Britain. He had every reason to look to the future with confidence. Then, in a matter of days, he found himself in a new world, where barbarism supplanted dreams and death could come at any hour. The Nazis demanded submission, but Karski found their cruelty beyond comprehension and so was among those who refused to collaborate or submit; he would resist. But for the Polish Underground to operate effectively, its members had to be able to communicate with one another. That meant developing ways to avoid detection while shielding the network from exposure in the event of arrests, which were inevitable. Karski, with his steady nerves and skill with languages, quickly established himself as the organization's principal international courier. In that role he employed all the tools of espionage: code names, forged documents, falsified personal histories, disguises, clandestine signals, and secret intermediaries. To the modern reader such a list might imply a certain glamor, but as Karski observed in his memoir, "The kind of work we engaged in had to be done by the simplest, most prosaic methods. Mystery and excitement attract attention and perhaps the greatest law of Underground work is: 'Be inconspicuous.'"[2]

The Underground's capacity to sustain itself depended on preserving the physical and psychological health of its members—no easy task. Karski and his fellow patriots subsisted on meager wartime rations at a time when bread flour was frequently mixed with sawdust, coffee was made from grain, butter and fresh vegetables were merely memories, and no consumer product was more coveted than lice medicine. But the scarcity of food and the abundance of vermin were less hazardous than despair. To Karski, the sight of his native land in chains was agonizing, as was the misery of friends who had lost loved ones, homes, jobs, savings, and hope. The Polish Underground was a stirring example of human resilience, but it provided no guarantee against personal desolation. Karski witnessed the self-inflicted death of a Polish officer, another young man paralyzed by fear, a Jewish leader who could not live with the knowledge of what was happening to his people, and a widow—Karski's own sister—who turned away from him when sorrow engulfed her heart. Even he, with his great reserves of determination, was driven at one point to attempt suicide.

As a messenger, Karski was regularly on the run either within Poland or between there and the Allied headquarters in Western Europe. These expeditions demanded from him both enormous mental discipline and physical stamina. He often had to bide his time for days, waiting for the right moment to make his next move while exposed to the elements or concealed in a wretchedly uncomfortable hiding place. Ordinarily a self-reliant person, he had to place his life in the hands of frontier guides who spent the war shepherding spies, escaped prisoners, soldiers, Jews, and other refugees out of the shadow of the Third Reich. Their perilous journeys—on foot or by bicycle, boat, truck, or skis—might consume a few hours or a few weeks, but as soon as one group reached its destination, another took its place in the queue. The guides were resourceful men and women whose judgment was tested each day and whose lives were constantly at risk. If a guide made a mistake or was betrayed, those with him would almost surely be captured. That is what happened to Jan Karski during one of his trips between Poland and France. Seized by the Gestapo, he was interrogated and had his teeth punched out, ribs broken, and hands lacerated before being knocked unconscious, then beaten again. His story might have ended there but did not. The description of his rescue is one of the more gripping sequences in this memorable play.

Members of the Polish Underground were battling to preserve their country's very existence and the right of their people to an independent state. To have any hope of prevailing, they needed both an internal political wing and leaders on the outside who had a platform from which they could openly plead the nation's cause. Karski's job was to serve as a human telephone line between the government-in-exile in the West and the freedom fighters in Poland. His success in that mission was due to far more than his ability to smuggle documents on microfilm; he was also a sharp-eyed and articulate observer with a nearly photographic memory. His reporting went beyond bare facts to include descriptions of atmosphere, morale, competing opinions, personal details, and whole conversations. These attributes were prized because the Poles under Nazi occupation were hungry for every scrap of news from the outside, and those in exile were full of questions about events back home.

The story of Jan Karski has in common with other tales of wartime resistance a richness of drama, human passion, and narrow escapes. What sets it apart is the man's uncompromising commitment to truth, the whole truth. This trait was most evident when, in mid-1942, the leaders of the Underground asked him to deliver their first fully comprehensive report and appeal to the West. By this time Karski had already escaped from enemy hands on two occasions and the odds against him were lengthening. The Nazis had locked down virtually all of continental Europe, including the former safe haven of France. The chances of his successfully carrying a message from his starting point in Warsaw to London were slim. With this daunting task before him, Karski could have been expected to gird himself quietly for the ordeal ahead and to do nothing that might add to the danger. Yet the courier's mind was uneasy. He was the one who had been chosen to bear witness. This meant that, before departing, he must see all there was to see.

So, in those hot summer days, Karski educated himself about the population many others wished to forget. Guided by friends and wearing the Star of David on his shirt, he went twice to the Jewish Ghetto in Warsaw. There he saw a community sealed off from the rest of the city, massively overcrowded and starving, a place where corpses were left to rot in the street because families could not afford the burial tax. Karski then went further, traveling by train and hay cart to a Nazi-run transit camp located 150 miles southeast of Warsaw. Disguising himself as a prison guard, he observed the loading of Jews into a cattle train for the short trip to an extermination facility. By then Karski's skin had grown thick; he had seen cruelty and death in abundance and felt he could control his emotions. He was objective, he assured himself, merely an observer, with no more human feeling than a camera. Yet the hardened spy became physically ill at what he saw. Two words were seared into his consciousness: Remember this.

Weeks later, when Karski arrived in London after a tortuous journey, he recalled every horrific image and heartrending sound. His testimony, given directly to Anthony Eden, the British foreign secretary, was one of the first eyewitness accounts of Nazi atrocities to reach the West. Although his message did not have the transformative impact for which Jewish leaders had hoped and prayed, neither did it go unheeded. On December 17, 1942, a dozen Allied governments joined in a collective denunciation of German war crimes. Addressing a special session of Parliament, Eden declared:

I regret to have to inform the House that reliable reports have recently reached His Majesty's Government . . . that the German authorities . . . are now carrying into effect Hitler's oft-repeated intention to exterminate the Jewish people in Europe . . . in Poland, which has been made the principal Nazi slaughterhouse, the ghettoes established by the German invaders are being systematically emptied of all Jews except a few highly skilled workers required for war industries. None of those taken away are ever heard of again. The able-bodied are slowly worked to death in labour camps. The infirm are left to die from exposure and starvation or are deliberately massacred in mass executions. The number of victims of these bloody cruelties is reckoned in many hundreds of thousands of entirely innocent men, women, and children.[3]

Unsurprisingly, the German government denied these and similar allegations. Almost until the war's end, they claimed that Jews were being shipped not to their deaths but to benign work camps, family-friendly ghettos, and, in the case of my native Czechoslovakia, to Theresienstadt, a prison described by Germans as "a Jewish spa." When Karski arrived in London to deliver his report, I was five years old, living in the same city. My father was the head of broadcasting for the Czechoslovak government-in-exile. His news team repeatedly warned the Nazis not to execute Jews, but the power to enforce that warning would not be brought to bear until, for millions of victims (including more than two dozen members of my family), it was too late.

The Polish government-in-exile considered Karski's message so important that its leaders decided not to order him to return to Warsaw but instead sent him to America, where he met at the White House with President Franklin Roosevelt, spoke frequently in public, and wrote a widely circulated book detailing what he had seen.

For Karski, the German surrender in May 1945 was profoundly welcome but far from satisfying. By then the full magnitude of the

Holocaust that he had warned against was being exposed; the horror was immeasurable and made the Allied efforts to stop or mitigate it appear shameful in their inadequacy. As for Karski's beloved Poland, it was freed from Nazi domination only to be hijacked in a matter of months by Stalin and the Soviets, who used the presence of the Red Army in Central Europe to seize control of the government in Warsaw.

Without a free Poland to return to, Karski remained in the United States and, in 1954, became an American citizen. He earned his PhD from Georgetown University, where he taught for the next four decades, specializing in East European affairs and comparative government. After he retired I had the honor of teaching some of the same courses. But before that I remember him as a professor during the latter stages of his career. He was a lanky man with aquiline features and piercing eyes who carried himself with dignity and was always immaculately dressed. Despite the difference in our ages, we shared a deep interest in the countries on the far side of the Berlin Wall, where it often seemed that nothing new or good would ever happen. Then the Cold War ended and Karski's dream of a liberated Poland was finally realized, almost exactly fifty years from the night that he had first reported for duty as a second lieutenant in the Polish army.

Jan Karski's courage in bearing witness to the Shoah is celebrated in Israel, where he was made an honorary citizen and where a tree was planted in his name in Yad Vashem's Garden of the Righteous Among the Nations. Shortly after his death in 2000 a statue bearing his likeness was dedicated on the Georgetown campus. His valor has been recognized posthumously by the Senate of Poland and also by the United States, where, in June 2012, President Barack Obama awarded him the Presidential Medal of Freedom. Said Obama: "We must tell our children" about Jan Karski and about "how this evil was allowed to happen."

With the president's suggestion in mind, I cannot conclude this without reminding readers that the enablers of evil are not confined to one side of the Atlantic. In the period just before World

War II there arose a multidimensional pro-fascist network within the United States, spurred on by German agents, fueled by demagogic media personalities, enamored of the slogan "America First," and built on a foundation of antisemitism, racism, isolationism, and fear. This was no trivial movement. It had prominent allies in the private sector, on newspaper editorial boards, in Congress, and among senior military officers. It also had a strong popular base, appealing to citizens eager to cast blame on those they held responsible for the Great Depression, especially bankers and East Coast politicians and financiers. The movement trafficked widely in conspiracy theories, most particularly in the belief that Jews were plotting to dominate the globe and that Franklin Roosevelt was himself a Jew. The fascist sympathizers held huge public rallies and even started their own schools. Had Japan not attacked Pearl Harbor, there is a real possibility that, because of this movement, the United States would never have entered World War II. Think about that.

I cannot speak for Jan Karski, but I suspect that he was not among those who saw in his life an inspiring example of personal heroism. Events beyond his control forced him to make the only choices that seemed possible to him at the time. He had many friends and colleagues who made similar choices but did not survive. He called himself "an insignificant little man" and viewed the past with immense and unshakable sorrow. Yet the message he left for us all could not be more important or uplifting: there is no such thing as an insignificant human being.

The central theme of this play is that we all have both the power and the responsibility to serve truth. That power is inherent in each of us, and that obligation is timeless. Truth is in a constant battle with destructive falsehoods, damaging stereotypes, unfounded rumors, and efforts to deny the dignity and humanity of whole groups of men, women, and children. Were he still with us today, I expect that Jan Karski would urge us never to collaborate with or submit to any untruth but rather to resist lies and liars while taking care, in our ardor, to avoid falling into a comparable trap ourselves.

That is a simple teaching but one well worth remembering because our willingness to put it more fully into practice may well determine not only our present-day happiness but also the collective future of our race.

Notes

1. Jan Karski, *Story of a Secret State* (Washington, DC: Georgetown University Press, 2014), 302.
2. Karski, 260.
3. 385 Parl. Deb. H.C. (5th ser.) (1942) 2082-7.

JAN KARSKI

A BRIEF BIOGRAPHY

Timothy Snyder

We would all like to imagine that we would have tried to stop the Holocaust. We would have crept into the ghettos to learn the truth, found our way to the Allied capitals, and made the case for action. We would have understood the annihilation of the Jews while it was happening and conveyed its horrors to the great and the good while there was time to act. Our social world would have included the suffering Jews and those with the power to change their fate; our war would have been one of conspiracy and concern. So, I suppose, we would all like to believe. The chances that any one of us would and could have behaved this way are about one in two billion. Of the two billion or so adults alive during the Second World War, only one of them achieved all of this: the Polish courier Jan Karski.

Karski was raised in the 1920s in the industrial city of Łódź— home at the time to as many Jews as was Palestine—and he studied with Jews at university in Lwów in the 1930s. He trained as an artilleryman in the Polish Army, a specialty where Jews were not at all prominent. But Jews, like everyone else in Poland, were subject to mandatory military service, and the armed services in interwar Poland were integrated. Karski then began a career in the diplomatic service, where Jews (with the exception of a few representatives of long-assimilated families) were not employed. As a young man he was a Catholic in faith and a patriot in his willingness to sacrifice for national independence.

The most important influence on young Karski was his older brother Marian, chief of the state police in Warsaw. When Germany invaded Poland on September 1, 1939, Marian was one of the relatively few Polish high officials to remain in the capital until it fell on September 27. Uncertain of what to do, he decided to ask the Polish government, reestablishing itself in exile in France. It seems that Marian decided to entrust his younger brother with this mission. By the time the two brothers met in Warsaw in October, Jan had already cheated death.

His war had begun at the Polish base at Oświęcim (better known as Auschwitz), where Polish troops were quickly overwhelmed by the German strike. Driven deep into the hinterland, they encountered the Red Army, which had invaded Poland from the east on September 17, 1939. Poland had been attacked from both sides, doomed by a secret German–Soviet alliance. Karski's commanding officers allowed the Soviets to disarm their units. Thus, as Karski recalled, "Polish men who, less than a month before, had left their homes to drive the Germans back to Berlin, were now being marched off to a nameless destination, surrounded by Soviet guns."[1]

By the end of September, Poland was doubly occupied, divided between a Nazi Germany and a Soviet Union that renewed their alliance with a Treaty on Borders and Friendship on the twenty-eighth of the month. In the lands of eastern Poland, the Soviets aimed to decapitate society by killing or deporting those Polish citizens with political pasts or notable ambitions. Their policy with prisoners-of-war was to release the enlisted men and keep the officers. Karski, who rightly sensed that something ill was afoot, managed to pass himself off as a simple soldier from working-class Łódź. Since his hometown was now under German rule, he was released into German custody. Thus he escaped the Soviet mass shootings of Polish officers known as the Katyń massacres. About 22,000 Polish citizens taken captive in the same circumstances as

Karski were murdered by the Soviet NKVD. Karski himself was transferred to a German prisoner-of-war camp in Radom. When the Germans tried to send him from Radom to another camp, he jumped from the train and escaped. He made his way back to Warsaw and found his brother, through whom he made contact with representatives of the emerging Polish Underground.

In the autumn weeks of 1939, Karski impressed them with his reliability, his memory, and his capacity for analysis. All seemed to agree that Jan Karski was a perfect candidate for a mission to the government-in-exile. He first agreed to undertake a survey of conditions of both Soviet and German occupation. A journey back east was a fiasco. Karski did find his way back across the border, smuggled along with a group of Jews escaping the German occupation. But no one in Lwów, his old university town, would speak to him. The Soviet NKVD had already so thoroughly penetrated the Polish Underground that his contacts suspected that his mission must be a Soviet provocation. Karski then surveyed Polish territories incorporated into the German Reich. From family members and others he learned of daily humiliations and mass deportations. In January 1940 Karski departed for France by way of the Carpathian Mountains and Slovakia. He made such a good impression upon government ministers with his reports that he was entrusted with a crucial political mission: to persuade the major Polish political movements to take part in a cooperative underground state.

Thus his return mission to Poland placed Karski in the middle of Polish politics and made him many new contacts. He was no longer simply the client of his brother and a few groups in Warsaw; he was the mediator between a government-in-exile and a mass political society at home. His original purposes were soon obsolete: his brother and other political patrons in Warsaw were arrested and sent to Auschwitz—no longer a Polish army base but a German concentration camp. It was in some measure due to Karski's own talents that the underground state did indeed come into existence, as a kind of holding tank for a future democratic Poland. Both the government-in-exile and the political parties took for granted that the rapid defeat in September 1939 had discredited Poland's experiment with authoritarianism in the 1930s. Victory in the war was to be followed by democratic elections. In the meantime, the major parties were to support the government-in-exile in the attempt to establish, insofar as was possible, the normal institutions of statehood under conditions of German occupation (under conditions of Soviet occupation this was unthinkable).

In June 1940 Karski was to return to France to report on progress. This time he and his guide were caught by the Gestapo in Slovakia, and Karski was tortured. Afraid that he would break and tell what he knew, he slit his wrists. He awoke in a hospital in a Slovak city, tied to the bed but able to see a newspaper headline announcing the fall of France. But all was not quite lost. The Polish government had been evacuated to London, and Karski was transferred to a hospital in German-occupied Poland, in Nowy Sącz. One Underground activist posing as a doctor helped him to slip out a request for poison, which was brought to him by another dressed as a nurse. But before they let him die with his secrets, the local resistance wanted to try to free him. One night Karski heeded the calls of the workers at his window to jump. He leapt naked into the darkness and was caught, dressed, and carried to a boat. He spent the rest of 1940 posing as a gardener on a rural estate, recovering his strength.

In early 1941 Karski was recruited for propaganda work. In Kraków he listened to British radio broadcasts and translated them for the Underground press. Again and again, the Polish resistance was wracked by German arrests; Karski lost a friend to Buchenwald. He was in Kraków when the Germans betrayed their Soviet ally and invaded the Soviet Union that June. In late 1941 he returned to Warsaw, where he would work for perhaps the most noble institution of the Polish Underground, the Bureau of Information and Propaganda of the Home Army. It was staffed by outstanding Polish liberals and democrats, some of them of Jewish origin.

As Karski prepared himself in the summer of 1942 for another journey as a political courier—this time to London—he learned as much as he could about the Holocaust. For him, as for much of the Polish Underground, the shock of realization of the totality of German intentions came with the clearings of the Warsaw Ghetto that summer. Beginning on July 23, the Germans began to deport Jews to the gas chambers of Treblinka at a rate of several thousand per day. Within about two months, some 265,040 Jews were sent to be gassed, and another 10,380 or so were killed in the ghetto itself. In late August 1942, right in the middle of these mass actions, Karski entered the Warsaw Ghetto twice. The initiative to arrange his passage by a secret route in seems to have come from Leon Feiner, an activist of the Jewish socialist party known as the Bund. Karski crept into the ghetto through a tunnel that led to the headquarters of the right-wing Zionist Jewish Military Union. In the ghetto he spoke with Feiner as well as Menachem Kirschenbaum, a Zionist. Both men explained the mechanisms of mass murder and the German aim to exterminate the Jews. Knowing that no force within Poland was in a position to halt such a determined German policy, they asked Karski to demand action from the Allies. They proposed that German cities be bombed and ethnic Germans be killed in open reprisals. They also told Karski to instruct Jewish activists abroad to conduct hunger strikes and to sacrifice their own lives to attract attention to the ongoing tragedy. Karski confirmed much of what he had seen and heard by daringly smuggling himself into the transit ghetto at Izbica Lubelska through which Jews were sent to the death facility at Belzec.

After mass one Sunday morning in September 1942, Karski departed for London, arriving in October. His political mission was to inform the Polish government about the state of Underground activity in Poland, but his personal priority was to communicate the reality of the Holocaust. He conveyed what he had seen and understood to the Polish prime minister and president with the request that the Vatican also be informed. Polish diplomats *did* inform the Pope about the Holocaust, to no effect. The Polish government had been reporting to its allies and the BBC about the Holocaust since the spring of 1942 and during the

Warsaw deportations issued an unambiguous statement about the Holocaust: "This mass murder has no precedent in the history of the world, every known cruelty pales in comparison."[2] Unlike the Polish government, Karski made no attempt to subsume the Holocaust within a larger account of the suffering of Polish citizens. In the weeks that followed he spoke to the American ambassador in London and virtually every significant British public intellectual. Neither the British nor the Americans responded to the pleas from the Jews of Warsaw for some immediate action to stop the Holocaust. The American ambassador found it unlikely that the United States would increase immigration quotas.

Karski also conveyed the message of the Warsaw Jews to Jewish leaders in London, including Szmul Zygielbojm, a member of the National Council of the Polish government-in-exile. Not long thereafter, in January 1943, the Germans tried to deport several thousand more Jews from the ghetto and met armed resistance. The Jewish Underground in Warsaw then began to plan for an uprising. When the Germans entered the ghetto again on April 19, Jewish fighters drove them out by force. On the roof of the building into which Karski had been smuggled the previous August, Jews raised two flags: the Star of David alongside the Polish flag. Alone in the world, with little help from the Polish Underground and no help from anyone else, the remaining Jews of Warsaw fought the Germans for more than a month.

On May 4, 1943, the Polish prime minister issued this unambiguous appeal: "I call on my countrymen to give all help and shelter to those being murdered, and at the same time, before all humanity, which has for too long been silent, I condemn these crimes."[3] By then the Germans were moving from block to block, burning out Jews from their bunkers with flame throwers. On May 12, Zygielbojm committed suicide, leaving a note: "Though the responsibility for the crime of the murder of the entire Jewish nation rests above all upon the perpetrators, indirect blame must be borne by humanity itself."[4] For the rest of his life Karski felt the weight of responsibility for Zygielbojm's death.

In April 1943, during the Warsaw Ghetto uprising, the Soviet Union broke diplomatic relations with Poland, even though both were fighting Nazi Germany. The tide of the war had now turned, and Stalin no longer had any need to pretend to respect the legal Polish government. His pretext for seeking to discredit it was the German revelation of the mass shooting at Katyń, where the Soviet NKVD had killed thousands of Karski's brother officers in 1940. The Soviets naturally blamed the Germans, a version that the British and Americans found most convenient to endorse. The Poles could hardly accept this lie, and they called for an independent investigation. Thus Stalin used the revelation of his own crimes against Poland as the justification to end official contact with the Polish government. It was perhaps this that prompted Karski's visit to Washington, DC, in June 1943.

Poland began the war under double German–Soviet occupation, then was occupied entirely by Germany, and finally would be occupied entirely by the Soviet Union. Karski's mission was to build sympathy for Poland on the basis of Poland's resistance to the Nazis and to help the Americans understand the danger of the Soviets. But, as before, he treated it as his personal responsibility to inform everyone who mattered about the course of the Holocaust.

In a meeting with Franklin D. Roosevelt that July, Karski informed the American president, unbidden, that millions of Jews had already been murdered, that the mass extermination of the Jews was a crime of a different order than the persecution of Poles, and that the Jewish nation would cease to exist without immediate Allied intervention. At this point about a hundred thousand Jews in Karski's native Łódź were still alive, and the large gas chambers at Auschwitz had only just become operational. Karski passed on Feiner and Kirschenbaum's request for retaliation against Germans. Roosevelt did not pursue the subject. In America as in Britain, Karski spoke to leading politicians and public figures about the Holocaust and once again had the impression that no one grasped the mechanics of the goals of the Final Solution.

After all of these appearances, Karski's career as a secret courier was obviously over. So in early 1944, during a second stay in Washington, Karski composed the book *Story of a Secret State*, reissued by Georgetown University Press in 2014. Written to improve the image of Poland and to gain American support for Poland in a coming conflict with Soviet power, the book was an exercise of a rather different sort than Karski's previous reports as a courier. As he was dictating the book in a New York hotel room to translator Krystyna Sokołowska, the Red Army was crossing into Polish territory for the second time during the war. So in describing his exploits, Karski had to protect not only all of his living contacts but all of the Underground's methods, since what remained of it would have to confront the NKVD.

In all of his communications, whether in conversation, confidential reports, or his bestselling book, Karski was perfectly consistent on one issue: the unprecedented character of the Holocaust of the Jews. As he concluded, "Never in the history of mankind, never anywhere in the realm of human relations did anything occur to compare with what was inflicted on the Jewish population of Poland."[5] To us today this seems so straightforward that we might forget that Karski's message went unheeded in London and Washington. In the middle of the war, no one in any Allied capital wanted to give the impression that it was being fought for the Jews. As the war came to an end, Karski had difficulty explaining the dangers of Soviet rule to American Jewish audiences, who correctly understood the arrival of the Red Army as the only hope for the survival of fellow Jews in Europe. Soviet propaganda did its part by calling Karski an antisemite. Then the Cold War began, Karski went to work for the American side, and the wartime history of Poland fell into the shade of the Iron Curtain.

In our own post–Cold War world, in which the Second World War becomes a site of wishful moralization about the Holocaust and much else, Karski remains a marginal figure, though for another reason. His incontestable heroism reminds us that the

Allies knew about the Holocaust but were not much interested. Karski recalls our weaknesses, one of which is that we forget them.

Notes

1. Jan Karski, *Story of a Secret State* (Washington, DC: Georgetown University Press, 2014), 15.

2. Quoted in Timothy Snyder, *Black Earth: The Holocaust as History and Warning* (New York: Random House, 2015), 264.

3. Quoted in Timothy Snyder, *Bloodlands: Europe between Hitler and Stalin* (New York: Basic Books, 2012), 291.

4. Quoted in Snyder, *Bloodlands*, 292.

5. Karski, *Story of a Secret State*, 302.

A PRODUCTION HISTORY

The Laboratory for Global Performance and Politics first presented an early version of *Remember This: The Lesson of Jan Karski* as a staged reading written by Clark Young and Derek Goldman and directed by Goldman in April of 2014 at Georgetown University to commemorate the centennial of Jan Karski's birth. David Strathairn portrayed Karski along with an ensemble of students from Georgetown's Department of Performing Arts. The original ensemble included Maria Edmundson, Peter Fanone, Greg Keiser, Walter Kelly, Ben Prout, Shannon Walsh, and Addison Williams.

In November of 2014 a second reading was staged at Teatr IMKA in Warsaw, Poland, in conjunction with the opening of POLIN Museum of the History of Polish Jews, built on the site of the Warsaw Ghetto. Strathairn worked with an ensemble of students from the National Academy of Theatre Arts in Kraków in a week-long workshop that culminated in two public performances.

The play continued its development with Strathairn and professional actors for multiple staged readings in December 2014 at Theater Row in New York and the Gonda Theatre at Georgetown University.

In June and July of 2015 the play had a multiple-week developmental residency at the Museum of Jewish Heritage in New York, including seven sold-out performances of the play as a workshop/

staged reading with Strathairn and a professional cast as well as an additional sold-out performance at Shakespeare Theatre Company's Sidney Harman Hall in Washington, DC, in partnership with the United States Holocaust Memorial Museum. The play also workshopped at the McCarter Theatre Center in Princeton, New Jersey, in 2016.

In November 2019 the one-man production of *Remember This: The Lesson of Jan Karski* was realized with a full staging in Gaston Hall at Georgetown University to commemorate the centennial of Georgetown's School of Foreign Service. In January 2020 the production was hosted at the People's Palace at Queen Mary University in London in partnership with Human Rights Watch for a sold-out performance to commemorate Holocaust Remembrance Day and the seventy-fifth anniversary of the liberation of Auschwitz.

The production received invitations to perform at leading festivals and theaters around the world, including in Edinburgh; Spoleto; Washington, DC; and throughout Poland, but these performances were postponed due to the COVID-19 pandemic. Plans are in place for the theatrical production to resume performances in 2021 at leading venues including the Shakespeare Theatre Company in Washington, DC.

In attendance at the production in London was documentary filmmaker Eva Anisko, an Emmy Award–winning film producer, who approached The Lab about adapting the play into a feature film. In the summer of 2020, the film was shot in black and white in a studio in Brooklyn, codirected by Jeff Hutchens and Derek Goldman. Anisko and her producing team plan to release the film in 2021–22.

Additionally, The Laboratory for Global Performance and Politics launched a course and accompanying educational platform built around the play and film, piloted at Georgetown University in the fall of 2020. The course features an experiential web-based platform that includes not only the filmed theatrical production but archival clips and interviews with leaders and key figures who engage with Karski's legacy. Titled Bearing Witness: The Legacy of Jan Karski Today, the course, created by Goldman and Young along with The Lab's inclusive pedagogy specialist Ijeoma Njaka, aims to allow students to articulate their own applications of bearing witness in local, national, and global contexts as they follow Karski's example to "shake the conscience of the world."

PLAYSCRIPT

REMEMBER THIS

THE LESSON OF JAN KARSKI

Featuring David Strathairn

By Clark Young and Derek Goldman

Directed by Derek Goldman

Produced by The Laboratory for
Global Performance and Politics

Adapted into the film *Remember This*

Directed by Jeff Hutchens and Derek Goldman

Produced by Eva Anisko

A space with a desk and two chairs.

A man addresses the audience.

MAN

We see what goes on in the world, don't we?

Our world is in peril. Every day, it becomes more and more fractured, toxic, out of our control. We are being torn apart by immense gulfs of selfishness, distrust, fear, greed, indifference, denial.

Millions are being displaced, impoverished, denied justice simply because of who they are, beaten, murdered, silenced, forgotten.

We see this, don't we? How can we not see this?

So what can we do? What can you do? What can I do?

What can we do that we are not already doing?

Do we have a duty, a responsibility, as individuals . . . to do something, anything?

And how do we know what to do? How do we know what we are capable of?

It's not easy—knowing.

Human beings have infinite capacity to ignore things that are not convenient.

*Human beings have infinite capacity to ignore things
that are not convenient.*

A clip plays from Claude Lanzmann's documentary Shoah.

In the clip, after a silence, Jan Karski tries to speak and breaks down:

"Now . . . now I go back . . .
Thirty-five years.
No . . . I don't go back.
As a matter of . . .
Alright.
I come back."

Jan Karski leaves the frame. The clip ends.

"No . . . I don't go back."

MAN begins to get dressed.

Jan Karski.
Born Jan Kozielewski, 1914.
Messenger of the Polish People to Their Government-in-Exile.
Messenger of the Jewish People to the World.
The Man Who Told of the Annihilation of the Jewish People While
There Was Still Time to Stop It.
A Hero of the Polish People.
Professor. Georgetown University, 1952 to 1992.

MAN becomes Jan Karski.

And always immaculately dressed.

And always immaculately dressed.

Now I go back . . .

In my classes on government and politics I tell my students . . .

He steps forward, as if addressing a classroom of students.

Governments have no souls. They have only their interests in mind.

What is your duty as an individual?

Individuals have souls.

The common humanity of people, not the power of governments, is the only real protector of human rights.

So I ask you: What is your duty as an individual? Every generation takes up a new revolution.

Szmul Zygielbojm. Remember his name. This man loved his people more than he loved himself. Zygielbojm shows us this total helplessness, the indifference of the world.

What we are witnessing now is very discouraging. Every generation brings destruction, partition, violence, and yet there is this desire to preserve language, identity, culture.

As a boy in Poland, we had to learn many languages because we never knew who would take us over!

///

For thirty-five years . . . I have never mentioned, even to my students, that I took part in the war.

I wanted to forget that degradation, that humiliation, that dirt.

I was forgotten, and I wanted to be forgotten.

One day, in 1978, I am discovered.

He knocks on the desk.

A man knocks on my door. A filmmaker.

His name is Claude Lanzmann. He is very full of himself . . . he likes to brag . . .

(as Lanzmann)
"I am making a film. It will be the greatest film ever made about the tragedy of the Jews. It will be called *Shoah*, and it will be as long as it needs to be to tell what needs to be told. Professor Karski, you will be in this film. There will be no actors. No Hollywood nincompoops. Only perpetrators, victims, witnesses. You are in the third group. I will have an interview with you."

(to Lanzmann)
"You will not have an interview with me. I'm out of it."

I remember, he is a bit of an authoritarian, he is very pushy . . .

(as Lanzmann)
"Professor Karski, look at the mirror. You are an old man . . . You are going to die soon. You have an historical responsibility. It is your duty to speak."

He convinces me.

I made a fool of myself . . . I broke down a few times. It was the first time I was involved again in that experience.

My wife, Pola, she can't stand it. We never discuss the war.

(as Pola)
"Jan, you torture yourself. You have done your job. It does you no good."

She leaves the house, walks for four hours. She's a dancer; she never stays still.

Lanzmann asks me questions . . .

(as Lanzmann)
"Do you think you succeeded in your report to the world?

Do you think you succeeded in conveying the magnitude?

Professor Karski, you are a unique witness. You are a hero . . ."

(to Lanzmann)
"No, no . . . I am an insignificant, little man. Hero? No!"

People in Poland were not happy I participated in that film. They say it does not reflect kindly on my country . . .

I am an insignificant, little man. Hero? No!

///

I was born in Łódź. At that time, one of the most multicultural cities in all of Europe, where, whether you are happy or unhappy, you always hear bells.

I remember, my grandmother gives me a bicycle.

(as Grandmother)
"Jasiu," she says. "Take this. See the Polish countryside, as it is now."

I ride east to west. Everywhere I go . . .

(as Poles Passing By)
"Witam! Witam, Jasiu." "Dzień Dobry!" "Powodzenia!" Good luck.

By American standards, we are rather poor. My father, Stefan Kozielewski, has a small factory producing saddles, women's bags, leather goods . . . I barely remember him; he dies when I am very young.

My mother, Walentyna Kozielewska, wants me to be a diplomat, an ambassador of Poland. I work hard. I listen. Everyone says I have an excellent memory . . . I am a good boy.

My mother is very, very Catholic . . . devotion, respect for others. She is making us in her image . . .

I remember, she tells me that when they took me to be baptized . . . my father, my godfather, my priest—all of them were drunk. She is disgusted, but this is Poland. In America, people drink to be in a better mood. In Poland, we drink to get drunk.

Now, I think every conversation would be better with a Manhattan.

///

In our apartment house, I remember, in the yard, some boys, children—whom my mother calls "bad boys." They would sneak and over the roof they would throw dead rats.

(as Mother)
"Bad boys. Bad Catholic boys teasing the Jews. Throwing dead rats at the Jews. Jasiu, keep watch, like a good Catholic boy. Go to the sukkah, where the Jews pray, and watch.

"Go to the sukkah, where the Jews pray, and watch."

If someone comes, simply call, 'Mamo, mamo.' I will take care of them."

And I watch.

///

My best friends at school are Jewish.

They help me in science. I help them in Polish literature, history.

Izio Fuchs, extremely religious. Everybody calls him a Jewish prophet. He starts every sentence, "I say."

Another one, Lejba Ejbuszyc. Abject poverty, a fighter. Full of resentment, hatred. He must have been badly treated.

Izio tells us . . .

(as Izio)
"I say . . . we have to be friendly to Lejba because if he doesn't find friends with us, where will he find friends?"

Izio's younger brother, Salus. Everybody likes Salus, but I like him most of all. He wants to be a pianist. But I can never get him to play the piano for me.

I don't know what happens to them.

My mother always says . . .

(as Mother)
"Jasiu. Climb the ladder. Nothing will stand in your way. Go. Go."

I leave Łódź for University to study law and diplomacy.

///

After graduation, I am invited to attend a youth rally . . . in Germany.

The enormous roar of a crowd.

Thousands of faces, all somehow the same. Tremendous hulla-baloo. Tremendous hall, like a concert, a circus. Darkness, shock. Nothing is happening. Then the sun descends on one point alone. A man, medals on his chest, light glowing around him . . .

That is Hermann Goering.

(as Goering)
"You have to take responsibility for the human race! Because you belong to the superior race! We are destined to govern, to bring order to the world, to create a lasting peace! And only the honest, decent youth of Germany can make such peace. Seig Heil! Seig Heil! Seig Heil!"

The sound of the crowd echoes and dissolves.

What is happening? That was Goering.

It's enough to make someone dizzy, the noise, the lighting. But . . . I think . . . maybe they are superior—to govern the whole world is a pretty overwhelming proposition, yet it sounds like fun to them. Why couldn't I be born German, I wonder, so I could be superior too?

To me, at this moment, they represent Western civilization.

///

Why couldn't I be born German, I wonder, so I could be superior, too?

I go to Geneva to learn French, then London, to learn English, which is very, very difficult. I work a low-level job in the Polish embassy . . . but I feel . . . I have a longing for home.

Polish folk music plays.

One evening, I go to the theater. An evening of Polish folk dance.

Alone on stage, dancing, barefoot, a girl, a Polish girl of outstanding beauty . . .

Her name is Pola. A Polish girl named Pola. Pola Nirenska.

A girl in exile here, far from home . . . what story is she telling with such urgency, such freedom? I have never experienced this form of expression before.

Amazing. Beautiful.

The sound of applause.

///

I return to Poland, to Warsaw, and I join the diplomatic service. If my mother were still alive, she would have been very proud. I want to represent my nation. I love my country. I am a proud citizen of a big empire.

He removes a note from the desk.

A slip of paper . . . a secret mobilization order . . .

"The Polish Army needs you. Settle your affairs and report to the train station in two hours."

Sent to the German border in a crisp khaki uniform with unbridled optimism.

The sound of a train.

(as Polish Soldiers)
"Death to Hitler!"

"Niech żyje Polska!"

"Long live, Poland!"

"We can finish this alone."

The train stops.

A town called Oświęcim . . .

In German, Auschwitz.

Later, infamous, but now, 1939, just an ordinary place with a brilliant, cloudless sky.

September 1st.

5:05 in the morning. Time for a shave.

Lights and sound evoke the Blitzkrieg.

It comes out of nowhere. The Germans bomb our camp.

Men are dying. I retreat, crawl back to the station. I don't even know who's firing, who's on our side. Total devastation. Chaos.

The Blitzkrieg.

Total devastation. Chaos. The Blitzkrieg.

I see the destruction of everything I have believed in. Poland is strong. Poland is an empire. Poland is the whole world to me, and that whole world is destroyed. Everything I have believed in up till now no longer applies.

Poland loses the war in twenty minutes.

///

I walk . . .

A refugee.

It is summer. The heat is terrible.

We don't know where we are going. Thousands of us, with no place to go . . . who will take us in?

I try to walk on the softer sides of my feet . . . so blistered . . .

For fifteen days I walk.

I see tanks . . .

The hammer and the sickle.

The Soviets have entered Poland.

A Polish captain waves a white handkerchief.

They take us to a labor camp.

///

We sleep in a warehouse beneath the red star and a portrait of Stalin.

We shiver in the raw, autumnal wind. Barbed wire encircles us.

(as Russian Guard)
"Cold? Are you Poles cold? That is because your bones are hollow, and your blood runs weak. You exploiters, bloodsuckers, you will learn how to work in Russia.

Your back will ache. Your hands will bleed. Your fingernails will break open. But you will learn how to work."

*"Your hands will bleed. Your fingernails will break open.
But you will learn how to work."*

For four weeks, I learn how to work.

I see an opportunity. There's an exchange coming with the Germans.

Approach a Russian officer—

(to Russian Officer)
"Sir, the men have been speaking of an exchange."

(as Russian Officer)
"You don't like it here?"

(to Russian Officer)
"I love it here. I would like to stay here. But my wife is expecting. Our first child. I want to return to Łódź to be with her."

I'm sure he realizes I am lying. This, for me, is a lesson. There is no such thing as good nations, bad nations. Each individual has infinite capacity to do good, and infinite capacity to do evil. We have a choice.

I lie. I survive.

The others will be taken to the edge of a pit and shot in the head. Stacked neatly in mass graves. 22,000 in the massacre at the Katyń Forest.

///

Radom. A military base in occupied Poland. A model Nazi facility.

We eat tiny amounts of inedible food. We sleep on the cold, hard November ground. No overcoat. No blanket. Every day deaths come from exposure and disease.

I see how common and lightly regarded death can be.

(as German Officer)
"Polish swine. You are going to be taken to a labor camp where you will work. If you attempt to escape, you will be shot. If you create a disturbance, you will be shot. Load the swine on the train."

///

I see how common and lightly regarded death can be.

He climbs onto the desk, as if thrown on a train.

(to Polish Prisoners)
"Citizens of Poland. I am going to jump from this train.

The war is not lost. We are not defeated. Join me, if you're willing to take the risk. I need three men to lift me and throw me out at a point along the track where there are no lights."

"Citizens of Poland.
I am going to jump from this train."

(as Polish Prisoner)
"Why would we help you? The Germans will shoot the rest of us."

(to Polish Prisoners)
"We are young men! Some only eighteen. We must not spend our lives as German slaves.

Are you or are you not a Pole?!"

He jumps.

I jump from the train.

I am no . . . James Bond; I do what I have to do.

I escape.

///

Again, I walk.

One hundred miles.

Thousands along the road . . . silent, exhausted.

Everywhere devastation left by the Blitzkrieg.

///

Warsaw.

A shocking ruin of its former self.

Street after street . . . heaped with rubble and debris. Cafes, theaters, libraries, churches vanished as if they never existed. Graves for the dead improvised in parks and public squares.

There is no longer a Poland.

Yet, irrationally, some part of me believes a fragment still exists. Something must be occurring . . .

(as Polish Underground Leader)
"Jan. Not every Pole has resigned himself to fate. We must fight if we want to exist.

Walk through this door.

Come in, young man . . . come in . . .

We have no doubt that you are faithful . . . That you are a patriot . . .

We hear you know languages. You know your way around Europe. You have a photographic memory.

Read this paper. Memorize it. Then destroy it. You will have a new name. A new skin. A new mode of existence . . .

You will call yourself 'Witold Kucharski.' Poland needs you. Walk with us, brother. Join the Polish Underground."

There is nothing extraordinary about it; nothing at all romantic. It comes as the result of a simple raising of the right hand.

He raises his right hand.

(as Polish Underground Leader)
"In the name of the Motherland . . ."

(to Polish Underground Leader)
"In the name of the Motherland . . .

I swear before God, his Son, and the Holy Spirit . . .

That I will not divulge . . .

Any of the information . . .

Which I am about to receive . . .

I swear to God . . .

That even under the most extreme circumstances . . .

Even unto death . . .

I shall remain faithful to the Polish nation."

(as Polish Underground Leader)
"By the oath you have just taken, you are now a member of the Polish Underground."

"By the oath you have just taken, you are now a member of the Polish Underground."

///

I become a tape recorder. A camera. A messenger . . .

My first mission . . . to see the Polish countryside as it is now.

To collect information in Łódź, Lublin, Belzec. Then proceed to France and report there to our government-in-exile.

I will report what I see.

The "Horst Wessel Song," a Nazi Party anthem, plays in the distance.

Łódź. December 1939.

All the streets, shops, offices have only German names and are flooded with German flags, slogans, posters. Poles cannot travel by automobile; they are even forbidden to own a bicycle. No matter where you turn, you hear only the German language. Łódź is no longer Łódź. Łódź is Litzmannstadt.

I report what I see.

He travels.

Lublin.

A lesson is taught, German to Jew, in gymnastics and hygiene.

Dozens of men, women, and children forced to sing those humiliating Nazi songs.

Doused with cold water in the freezing weather.

People faint from shock and exhaustion.

Young boys are stripped naked, mocked, and abused by the guards.

I report what I see.

He travels.

Belzec.

The Germans have created a camp of Jews.

All are frozen, in despair, unable to think, hungry. This has been going on for weeks.

I report what I see.

January 1940. My report.

The situation, the Jewish problem in the Homeland, is clear, uncomplicated, and easy to understand. Polish Jews, at least in the Western area, are intended for destruction or removal.

The Polish government does not release my report to the public.

///

Next mission. The mountains of Slovakia. Fifteen miles to safety . . .

He stops.

I'm tired of walking, but my guide says . . .

(as Guide)
"We must keep moving. Gestapo are everywhere on the lookout."

(to Guide)
"But my feet are swollen. I must get some rest . . ."

We reach a humble cottage.

///

Three a.m. . . .

(as Nazi Soldiers)
"Hands up!"

"Where's your knapsack?"

"Are you hiding anything?"

(to Nazi Soldiers)
"No . . . no . . ."

A strike.

They break my jaw.

A strike.

Fists and truncheons. Teeth spilling from my mouth. Broken ribs.

A strike.

They are beating me . . . for two days, "Tell us. Tell us." . . . Hoses behind my ear. My genitals. Beating me, beating me, beating me within an inch of my life.

He collapses.

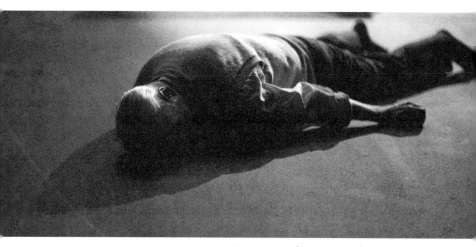

*Beating me, beating me, beating me
within an inch of my life.*

///

Bells. After a moment, a memory.

(as Teacher)
"Jasiu, Jasiu, you have something to share? Jasiu, your classmates
are waiting."

(to Teacher)
"A poem by Mickiewicz."

(as Teacher)
"Do you need your paper?"

(to Teacher)
"No. I remember . . .

He closes his eyes and recites a small portion of "The Pilgrim."

A tragic, lonely terror grips my heart
A longing for some peaceful, gentle place
And memories of youthful love I trace
Unto my childhood home I long to start."

///

The sound of cell doors closing.

A resplendent Nazi youth enters my cell.

(as Nazi Officer)
"Witold Kucharski.

We don't usually get your type here. You have culture and breeding. If you had been born German, you would be very much like I am. Brandy? Cigarette?

"If you had been born German,
you would be very much like I am."

I know who and what you are. You're carrying information from the Underground to your leaders in France. You must enable us to get in touch with your authorities. If you love your country, you will not reject this proposition.

Very soon the Fuhrer will dictate peace in London. In a few years he will proclaim the New Order on the steps of the White House in Washington. This new peace will be permanent. We don't want to harm anybody. With the exception of the Jews, of course. They will be exterminated. For your loyalty to the Third Reich, we will permit participation in our new civilization.

Do you accept my proposal?"

(to Nazi Officer)
"I am an insignificant, little man. You have overestimated my importance."

(as Nazi Officer, rising to strike)
"You are nothing but a dirty, little coward.

Polish swine!"

A brutal beating.

(to Nazi Officer)
"No . . ."

He collapses.

///

Bells. Another memory. He receives communion.

(as Priest)

"Jasiu. This is an offering of peace and safety. Not everyday safety, but the most supreme safety, safety in God.

I present you, child of Poland, with Christ's Body, to carry with you on your journey. It will protect you from all evil and harm."

///

The sound of cell doors closing.

I cannot take anymore. I know too much. All the names. All the addresses. I swore I would never break, never disgrace my Poland.

Here, I die a wretched, inglorious death, like a crushed insect. Family, friends will never even learn what has happened, where my body will lie . . .

In my shoe I have concealed a blade.

He gestures as if cutting his wrists.

Plunge the blade into my right wrist. My beloved motherland, I love you . . .

Saw back and forth. My beloved motherland, I love you . . .

Slam the wrist down onto the blade. My beloved motherland, I love you . . .

Thrash! Thrash! My beloved motherland, I love you . . .

I am trying to cut my veins, but it's not so easy. They are very hard, the veins. The blood is running—then it stops. So I am . . . waving, waving, waving . . .

My beloved motherland, I love you.

I fail.

He falls on the desk.

///

Let me die. Please. Let me die . . .

(as Polish Nurse)
"Shhh . . . don't be frightened. You are in a Polish hospital.

The Gestapo don't want you dead. They brought you here. They think you will break. They'll come back, but we will not abandon you.

Poland still needs you. You're going to be set free tonight.

We've bribed the guard. At midnight, a doctor will pass this room and light a cigarette. Take off your gown and move down the corridor. You'll find a rose on one of the windowsills. Jump from that sill. Men will be stationed below. Is everything clear?"

(to Polish Nurse)
"I understand."

A clock chimes.

The church clock tolls midnight.

He undresses.

Look, a figure.

A shadow.

A match.

A cigarette.

The signal.

A draft of cold air . . .

The rose.

The window is open.

Now is the time.

Jump.

Jump.

(as Polish Underground Member)
"Jump!

What are you waiting for?!

JUMP!"

He jumps.

(as Polish Underground Member)
"Get him to the water."

Thrown into a canoe. Wrapped in a freezing blanket. All I hear—
paddling, paddling . . .

(as Polish Underground Member)
"End of the line, Witold. This is where we separate. No more contact. You'll spend some time away. An old estate. It's nice there."

(to Polish Underground Member)
"Thank you . . ."

(as Polish Underground Member)
"Don't be too grateful. We had two orders. The first was to help you
escape. The second was to shoot you if we failed.

You were lucky."

The ones who save me . . . thirty-two Poles, doctors, nurses, are
tortured by the Germans all summer long.

No one gives in.

So they are lined up and shot to death.

///

He slowly gets dressed.

A small farm in the Polish countryside.

I breathe the clean, fresh air.

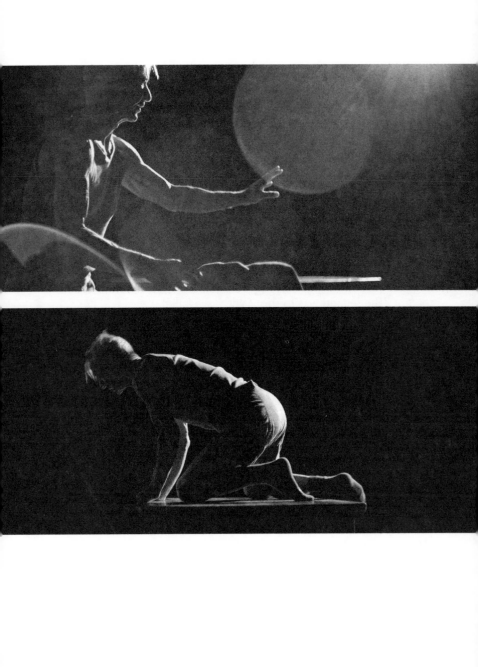

"What are you waiting for?! JUMP!"

I melt into the landscape.

I pretend to be a gardener. I hardly recognize myself.

Seven months of healing.

I regain my strength.

He looks at his wrist.

Even in the heat, now, I always wear sleeves.

I am restless. In my sleepless nights, I listen to love songs on the gramophone.

Distant music plays.

And I read Kafka.

"Far, far from you, world history is unfolding, the world history of your soul . . ."

. . . The world history of my soul . . .

Governments have no souls . . . Individuals have souls.

He starts to put on his shoes.

The barefoot dancer in London . . .

The Polish girl, Pola Nirenska—she, too, was far from home, always moving.

I am useless here. I must do something.

The world history of my soul . . .

The Polish resistance is growing. The Nationalist Party, Socialist Party, Peasant, Christian Labor.

I return to work. To carry their messages.

They are sending me to London to report to the Allied Nations. The Allies must know the Polish people are placing our hopes in them.

He removes a note from the desk.

Before I leave, a message . . .

The Jewish people have their own Underground. They have learned about my mission.

I agree to one last meeting.

///

An old house on the outskirts of Warsaw.

Cold. Twilight.

I sit in an old, rickety armchair.

Two men, Jewish leaders, walking through the room—they do not give their names.

Nobody gives their names.

Less like men . . . incarnations of mass suffering and nerves.

Frustrated. Shouting.

(as First Jewish Leader)
"We know about you, Witold."

Whispering.

(as Second Leader)
"We know about you."

Walking, walking through the room . . . nightmarish.

(as First Leader)
"We know about you. We know you are going to London. We know you are carrying messages. The Jewish people have messages too."

(as Second Leader)
"He will not understand!"

(as First Leader)

"We know that in London and in Washington and in New York, it is impossible for them to believe what is happening to us, that they believe we are exaggerating, that we're hysterical.

They are not doing enough. We are being systematically murdered.

We cannot defend ourselves, and no one in Poland can defend us. This is what people do not understand.

Our representative in London is Szmul Zygielbojm. He tells us he's doing everything he can to help us. It's not enough. We're dying here. Let them do something that will force the world to believe . . ."

(as Second Leader)

"He doesn't understand!"

(as First Leader)

"Tell Zygielbojm the Jewish people must do something that will make the rest of the world believe us. We are all dying here. Let them die too. Let them crowd the offices of Churchill, Roosevelt, and all the Allies. They should stand in the streets and they should refuse to eat. They should refuse water. They should proclaim a hunger strike and die in view of all mankind. Let them die a slow death while the world is looking on."

(as Second Leader)

"No! He does not understand . . . His cities will be rebuilt. His wounds will heal.

What's the good of talking? No one in the outside world can possibly understand."

(as First Leader)

"From this ocean of tears, pain, rage, and humiliation, Poland will emerge again, Witold, but the Polish Jews will no longer exist. Hitler may lose his war against the Allies, and yet he will win his war against the Polish Jews.

Young man, it has never happened before in history. Egyptian pharaohs did not do it! Babylonians did not do it! We have very little time.

Unless the Allies take unprecedented steps, we will be totally exterminated."

A solemn proposition.

(as First Leader)

"We can organize for you to visit the Jewish ghetto. We can organize for you to visit a Jewish camp.

Mr. Witold, I know the Western world. I am sure it will strengthen your report if you are able to say, I saw it myself.

Of course, you may say no.

I will go with you. I will be sure that you will be as safe as possible. Who knows? Perhaps this will shake the conscience of the world . . .

Will you do it?"

He nods.

///

"Who knows? Perhaps this will shake the conscience of the world."

We enter the ghetto through this tunnel without any kind of difficulty. I am not disguised . . . He is not disguised.

I wear the Star of David. He puts it on me.

So we walk in the streets.

He is on my left. We do not talk very much.

///

So now comes the description of it, yes?

///

Naked bodies on the street. Corpses.

I ask him, "Why are they here?"

He says, "We have a problem, Mr. Witold. If a Jew dies and the family wants a burial, they have to pay tax on it. So they just throw them in the street."

Women publicly feeding their babies, but they have no breast, just flat. Babies with crazy eyes, looking.

This is not a world; it is not humanity. The streets full—apparently all of them live in the street. Everybody offering something to sell. Three onions, some cookies, selling, begging each other, crying, hungry. Some children running by themselves or with their mothers, sitting. It is not humanity; it is some hell.

We leave the ghetto.

He says . . . "You did not see everything. Will you go again? I want you to see everything."

Next day we go again. The same way.

Now I am more conditioned, so I notice other things.

The stench, the terrible stench everywhere, suffocating. Dirty streets . . .

Dirty streets, nervousness, tension . . . bedlam. This is Platz Muranovsky. In one corner children playing with rubbish, throwing rubbish to each other.

He says, "They are playing. You see? Life goes on, life goes on."

They are simulating playing. They don't play.

We just walk the streets. We do not talk to anybody. We walk probably for one hour. Sometimes he tells me—

"Look at this Jew."

A man standing there, without moving.

Is he dead?

"No, he is alive, Mr. Witold. But remember, he is dying, he is dying. Look at him. Tell them over there—in London, in the United States—you saw it. Don't forget."

We walk again.

Only from time to time he whispers . . .

"Remember this."

"Remember this."

"Remember this."

Only from time to time he whispers . . . "Remember this."

I ask, "What are they doing here?"

"They are dying. That's all right, they are dying. They are dying . . ."

And always, "Remember, remember, remember!"

Suddenly, some movement starts. People running from the street, fleeing. We jump into some apartment house. He pushes me to the window. "Look. Look," he says.

Two boys, nice-looking boys, Hitler Youth, soldiers, laughing, talking to each other in the street. Every step they make, people running, running, fleeing from them.

Suddenly one boy reaches to his hip pocket, a pistol. Without even thinking, takes aim. A target.

The sound of shattered glass.

A scream. "Ahhhhhh . . ." "Ahhhhh . . ."

The other boy says something, congratulating him. He pats him on the back, and they walk away.

A woman puts her hand on my shoulder . . . perhaps she recognizes that I am not a Jew . . . embraces me, says, "Go, go, it doesn't do you any good. Go, go."

This was not part of humanity. I was not part of it. I did not belong there. I had never seen such things . . . I never saw any theater. I never saw any movies. Nobody wrote about this kind of reality. I was told that these were human beings, but they did not look like human beings.

We leave the ghetto.

He says to me, "Witold, we've organized for you to visit a Nazi camp. You'll be in the company of a Ukrainian militiaman.

Powodzenia. Good luck . . ."

He tells me I will see something I have never seen and which I will never forget, and I am going to see a camp, actually a camp. A Jewish ghetto is not a camp. It is only degradation, a way to death. I am going to see a death camp now.

///

I enter the camp wearing the uniform of a Ukrainian. I remember the militiaman says something, "There is a new batch which is going to be processed today."

From the main gate there is . . . there is a cattle train. I count forty-six trucks.

There is this ramp, a platform, from the gate leading to the train, almost directly. On the train floor there is a whitish powder.

I ask the Ukrainian militiaman, "What is it?" He says, "It is for their hygiene. This is quicklime. So, when they die there is no problem, they will not contaminate the air whatsoever. Himmler said, 'The Jews will die, and they will die in agony. They will die. Don't worry, they will die.'"

In that part of the camp—and I do not know how many, it must be 5,000, 4,000, 6,000—this cannot be described. Not humanity. Crowds, some collective moving body, the Jews—women, children, men—shouting, quarreling with each other, fighting against each other. Evidently hungry. A man totally, completely naked, just standing. Why is he naked? I don't know. Perhaps he threw his clothes, perhaps some people took his clothes. Standing, in this agony . . .

At this time, I am strong.

I understand my mission. I am not supposed to have any feelings. I am a camera. There is a crowd, out of reality—a crowd which has many heads, legs, many arms, many eyes, but it is something like a collective, pulsating, moving, shouting body.

And I am observing this. I do not want to see them as humans. I control myself—I don't know, twenty minutes, half an hour . . . however long I stand there. I do not want to have any feelings. I do not have any feelings. I am just seeing something which I am supposed to report.

That horrible, horrible scene. Those shouts, despair, mothers dragging their children to the trucks, but they cannot reach, they are too weak.

Behind them, Gestapo, militia, pushing them, pushing, "Juden raus!" Beating them like pigs, like non-humans.

Starving, hungry, insane, mad—I see their eyes . . . some organism with heads, legs, arms, noses.

I control myself. I realize, again, with no feelings; look, no feelings; look, no feelings; look, look. But . . . I can't help it. It comes too deeply into me—humans! They are individuals here!

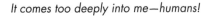

It comes too deeply into me—humans!

I lose control. I realize I don't know what I should do—I might jump some Gestapo and start fighting. I might go with the Jews to the train. I realize things are out of control with me.

I leave the camp.

He moves away.

I ask a storeowner, "Could I use your kitchen?" I am insane. I am crazy. I enter the kitchen, and as if in—I don't know—self-preservation, animal, I actually disrobe myself and start to wash myself with soap, everything. I am washing myself! I remember I am washing my shoes . . . I start to wash my shoes! Then the owner comes. I just ask him one question: "May I stay here tonight? I cannot go back." He says, "Sure, you can stay overnight."

You may consider what I say a sort of terrible ancient myth. Rather unreal. It's difficult to visualize. The mind cannot absorb that it is real, that it really happened. It becomes a myth.

All I can say is that I saw it, and it is the truth.

///

Twenty-one days to London.

All I can say is that I saw it, and it is the truth.

In disguise. A train takes me from Warsaw to Berlin, then Brussels, occupied Paris, then across the Pyrenees Mountains on foot in the snow, Madrid.

A plane takes me to London.

I report to Szmul Zygielbojm.

(as Zygielbojm)
"I was told you wanted to see me. What do you want?"

(to Zygielbojm)
"Mr. Zygielbojm, I don't want anything. I have messages."

(as Zygielbojm)
"Are you Jewish?"

(to Zygielbojm)
"No."

(as Zygielbojm)
"So, talk. Talk. You are here to talk, so talk."

I give him all the material.

Then . . . like with hatred, frustration . . . he says . . .

(as Zygielbojm)
"I know all this already. My family is there! You haven't told me anything I don't already know . . .

So, what can I do? What can I do that I am not doing? I do every-thing . . . I do everything that is possible, so what can I do?!"

I close my eyes and give it to him.

(to Zygielbojm)

"Jews are dying. There will be no Jews. What is the use of having Jewish leaders? Let the Jews go to the most important offices, Allied offices. Let them demand. If they are refused, let them go out, let them stay outside, let them refuse drink, let them refuse food, let them die, let them die a slow death, let humanity see it. Perhaps it will shake the conscience of the world."

And then, he jumps . . .

(as Zygielbojm)

"Madness, madness, madness. They are mad, they are mad. The whole world is mad. They are crazy, they don't understand anything, they will not let me die, they will send me to policemen, they will arrest me, they will take me to an asylum, they will feed me artificially. They are mad. Everybody's mad. So I have to do something . . . but I don't know what? So what can I do? I have to do it, but I don't know what? So what to do?

*"So I have to do something . . . but I don't know what.
So what can I do?*

This is a mad world. I have to do . . . I don't know what to do . . . so what do I do?!"

Now this may seem cynical, but, at this time, I am a machine. Twenty-eight years old. My life consists of moving from one contact to another. Eating, sleeping, reporting . . . All those I am reporting to are very important people, and I am an insignificant, little man. My mission is important.

Perhaps this shows that I am, in a way, morally corrupted, because in the second part of the meeting I am only thinking about one thing . . .

(to Zygielbojm)
"I'm sorry, Mr. Zygielbojm, but I am going to be late for my next appointment."

///

Six months in London. My own apartment. Evenings of air raid sirens, the Luftwaffe overhead.

Foreign Secretary Anthony Eden informs me that Polish reports of these atrocities have already reached them.

(as Eden)
"The matter will take its proper course," he says.

(to Eden)
"May I report to Prime Minister Churchill?"

(as Eden)
"No. I will not permit you to take his time."

When Churchill speaks to Parliament in 1946, he says that he had no idea of the scale of these horrible massacres which had occurred, the millions and millions who had been slaughtered.

That it dawned on him gradually after the war was over.

///

I am sent to America, secretly. I still remember the Statue of Liberty emerging from the New York Harbor.

In Washington I stay at the Polish embassy.

The Polish ambassador comes with Justice Felix Frankfurter.

A little man. He does emanate some brilliance. Very alive in his eyes. He calls me . . .

(as Frankfurter)
"Young man.

Young man, do you know who I am?"

(to Frankfurter)
"Yes, sir. You are Associate Justice of the Supreme Court."

Silence.

Frankfurter starts—

(as Frankfurter)
"Mr. Karski, young man, I have been invited by my very good friend, your ambassador, to come here to see you. I was also advised that

I should see you. Apparently you have some information which I should know. Young Man, do you know that I am a Jew?"

(to Frankfurter)
"Yes sir, Mr. Ambassador told me this."

(as Frankfurter)
"Well, tell me about the Jews. We have here many reports. What happens to Jews in your country?"

What happens to Jews in my country . . .

Now, I become a machine. The man sits. I report. Jewish leaders. Ghetto. Camp. Fifteen, twenty minutes pass. He doesn't interrupt. And I stop.

I remember, he looks . . . smaller and smaller . . . he is looking at the floor.

(as Frankfurter)
"Young Man, as I mentioned, I have been informed about your activities. I was told that you came out of hell. My admiration for people like you . . ."

And now . . .

(as Frankfurter)
"Young man, I am no longer young. I am a judge of men. Men like me talking with men like you must be totally honest. And I am telling you . . . I do not believe you."

Ambassador breaks in—

(as Polish Ambassador)
"Felix, what are you talking about? He was checked, rechecked hundreds of times. Felix! He is not lying."

(as Frankfurter)
"Mr. Ambassador, I did not say that he's lying. I said that I do not believe him. These are different things. And my mind, my heart . . . they are made in such a way that I cannot accept.

I know humanity. I know men. Impossible. No. NO! NO!!!"

"I know humanity. I know men. Impossible. No. NO! NO!!!"

///

He removes a letter from the desk.

(as Zygielbojm)
"Prime Minister Churchill. President Roosevelt.

In the name of the Jews who are being murdered in vast numbers behind the gates of the ghetto, I turn to your governments with this last desperate appeal. Of the three and a half million Jews from before the war, there now remain alive no more than a few thousand. The surviving Jews in Poland beg you to find the means to save them.

Try to imagine the people who see their loved ones being dragged away to their death every day and each one knows that their turn must come. Imagine the great crime of methodically massacring an entire people. The conscience of every person must be shaken by the greatest crime in human history. I call on all people to erase the burning shame that is directed at the human race—force the Nazi murderers to stop the systematic massacre of a people.

Szmul Zygielbojm."

///

"The conscience of every person must be shaken by the greatest crime in human history."

A limousine picks me up. Takes me to the most powerful man in the most powerful nation in the world.

The ambassador tells me . . .

(as Polish Ambassador)
"Johnny, you are inclined to talk too much. Poland is a minor concern for him. He has the whole world. Be precise."

Ambassador punctual . . . president punctual . . . secretary leads me to his office.

I see him.

He looks . . . like a world leader . . . yes, a world leader. As a matter of fact, it strikes me . . . he is more than the president of the United States.

I see a Lord of Humanity. A Lord of Humanity.

He sits behind his desk. Behind him, of course, all American flags . . . impressive, the whole wall covered by them. Very high chair.

I was warned he will not get up to shake your hand.

He shakes my hand.

(to Roosevelt)
"All hope, Mr. President, has been placed by the Polish nation in the hands of . . . Franklin Delano Roosevelt."

I am thinking how much time I have. I want to pin him down.

(to Roosevelt)
"Mr. President, I am returning to Poland. Every leader will know that I spoke to President Roosevelt. Sir, everybody will ask me—what did the President tell you? Mr. President, what do I tell them?"

(as Roosevelt)
"You will tell your leaders that we shall win this waaaaaar."

"You will tell your leaders that we shall win this waaaaaar."

. . . long cigarette, long cigarette holder . . .

(as Roosevelt)
"Win this waaaaaar. The guilty ones will be punished for their criiiiiiimes. Justice, freedom shall prevail. The United States will not abandon your country."

Now, I come to the Jewish problem.

(to Roosevelt)
"Mr. President. Before leaving Poland, I met with the most important Jewish leaders. They organized a visit in the ghetto. I saw a camp.

Mr. President, the situation is horrible. More than 1,800,000 Jews have been murdered in my country. I have brought with me the official declaration of my government: If there is no effort at Allied intervention within the year, the Jewish people of Poland will cease to exist."

And now he asks me questions . . . do you know the questions he asks me?

(as Roosevelt)
"Do I understand correctly, young man, that before the war Poland was essentially an agricultural country?"

(to Roosevelt)
"Yes, Mr. President. It was so."

(as Roosevelt)
"From what we understand of the Russian campaign, the Germans had to use a tremendous number of horses. Did they take those horses from Poland? Because with your agricultural economy, you need horses."

(to Roosevelt)
"Mr. President, yes."

He does not ask a single, specific question about the Jewish problem.

(as Roosevelt)
"Your story is very important. I'm glad I heard it. I'm sorry; I am a half-hour late for my next meeting. I wish you success and a happy return to your country. I hope you will come back to America."

///

I do not go back to Poland. I can't. I am deciphered. I am known, and I know too much.

When the war comes to its end, I learn that the governments, the leaders, the scholars, the writers say they did not know what was happening to the Jews, that the murder of six million Jews was a secret.

They knew. Public opinion knew at the time. The government knew. Intellectuals knew. Even if some didn't know, it was only because they didn't want to know. The Jewish problem was insignificant.

The Jews were left alone to perish.

My faith tells me the second original sin has been committed by humanity. Through commission or omission or self-imposed ignorance or insensitivity or self-interest or hypocrisy or heartless rationalization or outright denial, this sin will haunt humanity to the end of time.

It haunts me now, and I want it to be so.

///

He removes a second letter from the desk.

(as Zygielbojm)
"To His Excellency, the President of the Republic of Poland. Mr. Prime Minister.

I cannot continue to live and be silent while the remnants of Polish Jewry, whose representative I am, are being murdered. By my death, I wish to give expression to my most profound protest against the inaction in which the world watches and permits the destruction of the Jewish people.

My life belongs to the Jewish people of Poland, and therefore I hand it over to them now.

I yearn that what remains of the millions of Polish Jews may live to see liberation, together with the Polish masses. That this liberation shall be permitted to breathe freely in Poland, in compensation for the inhuman suffering and torture inflicted on the Jewish people. And I believe that such a Poland will arise and such a world will come about.

I take leave of you with greetings from everybody and from everything that was dear to me and that I loved.

Szmul Zygielbojm."

The suicide of Zygielbojm, May 11, 1943, for me, shows more than anything else the Jewish tragedy of the Second World War.

About him I speak.

He shows us this total helplessness, the indifference of the world, the indifference of the world!

I have not had one single class in all my years of teaching, when I come to the war situation, I do not tell my students, "There was Zygielbojm!!!"

There are voices still that say the Holocaust never happened, that it was an exaggeration. These voices are weak. They have no future.

Now I always dedicate one class to speak about what I saw.

"There was Zygielbojm!"

I tell my students we have a future because we are speaking the truth.

///

My wife, Pola, also a teacher . . .

That barefoot dancer in London, remember? I see her again, twenty years later, dancing in a Washington synagogue.

Remarkable.

I find her address, send a fan letter. "Would you like to go out on a date?" Nothing. A few weeks go by—I find her number. "Dinner?" "No," she says. "But I'll go to lunch."

A Jewish girl studying dance in Germany. Hitler came. She moved to Italy. Mussolini came. She goes to London, then Washington. Throughout the war, she never stopped dancing.

She taught in our home, our basement—we made a heated floor for her students, dancing. A happy and light atmosphere.

But she stopped . . . it was tiring, and she was not well . . .

But she was not done.

A final performance at the Kennedy Center.

She did not want me to go . . . but, of course, I am going.

Music.

"In memory of those I loved who are no more."

"In memory of those I loved who are no more."

Applause.

She had left her family in Poland. Seventy-two of them. They all perished.

Pola could only experience the Holocaust in her imagination.

He sat down on a bench and watched the people go by.

She took her life. A fall from our balcony.

. . . She would tell her students, "Look around. Notice people. Pay attention. Pull all reactions to them into choreography."

///

He begins to remove his suit.

When I left the White House on that day in 1943, President Roosevelt was still smiling and fresh. I felt fatigued. It was, however, not an ordinary fatigue, but more the satisfied weariness of the workman who has just completed his job with a last blow of his hammer, or an artist who signs his name under the completed picture. Something was coming to an end, and all that was left was this weariness.

He removes his shoes and becomes MAN again.

He sat down on a bench and watched the people go by.

They were well-dressed and looked healthy and complacent. They hardly seemed to be affected by the war. Events passed through his mind in quick, strange fragments. The ghetto and the death camp. The memory bringing nausea.

The whispered words . . .

Remember this . . . remember this . . . remember this . . .

///

What can we do? What can you do? What can I do?

Do we have a duty, a responsibility, as individuals . . . to do something, anything?

Karski said, "Great crimes start with little things . . . You don't like your neighbors. You don't like them because they are different. Avoid this. Avoid disliking people. Don't make distinctions."

But how do we know what to do; how do we know what we are capable of?

How do we know what to believe? How do we know what to believe in?

Is there something we can do that we are not already doing?

Is there something we can do that we are not already doing?

These questions haunt me now . . .

And I want it to be so.

MAN exits.

End of Play.

A CONVERSATION ON *REMEMBER THIS*

Derek Goldman, David Strathairn,
and Clark Young

Moderated by
Deborah Tannen

DEBORAH: I have to say at the start that I've been gobsmacked by what you've all created. And I've been watching from the beginning—that first staged reading at Gaston Hall, which Georgetown students took part in. David, you were the shining jewel in the crown of that. And then the various other incarnations of it. The amazing one-man show that I saw in Gaston Hall. And then the film, which I've now seen. I'm a theater fanatic, as Derek knows, so I was skeptical, but the film is astonishing. It is, in some ways, even more moving because the audience is so close to David's performance and Jan Karski himself. So, thank you, thank you, thank you for what you've created here.

I didn't know Jan Karski well, but he was a faculty member at Georgetown when I arrived. I remember the first time I was at a university-wide meeting, and he was there. A person sitting next to me pointed him out and whispered, "Do you know who that is?" I didn't, so she told me about his history. My father was born in Warsaw. So, I felt that connection. We are Jewish, but my father left shortly after the First World War. So, his wasn't a Holocaust story. But I did chat with Karski about that. What stuck in my mind, my name is Tannen, but my father's name in Poland was Tenenwórcel. Karski immediately recognized that name and said, "Oh, yeah, I knew lots of Tenenwórcels. That's a common name." That's the only time I got that reaction to my father's Polish name!

I've always been deeply moved that Karski's statue sits on the commemorative bench at Georgetown. It's the only statue I've ever seen of a person I knew. I feel fortunate that I pass by it whenever I walk from my office onto campus. Anyone who is unlucky enough to be looking at it when I'm walking by runs the risk that I'll stop and say, "Do you know who that is?!" And tell them the story. It's so meaningful that you've all created this, and it's such an amazing piece of work. Let's start by each of you saying how you became involved and how this whole thing came about. Derek, I guess that starts with you.

DEREK: I became involved in 2014, in the build-up to Georgetown's efforts to commemorate Karski's centennial year. I had, as you know, a deep history around the intersection of the Holocaust, specifically in Poland, and the arts with our production of *Our Class* and other Holocaust works. I was familiar with the outlines of Karski's story but had not done a deep dive into the full sense of the narrative of his life. And Scott Fleming, who was associate vice president for federal relations at Georgetown, initially reached out to me. Scott was part of the commemorative planning committee. He had known my theater work and said they were thinking of doing a theatrical piece about Karski. I certainly didn't have a full sense yet of all the dimensions and resonance, but pretty quickly I felt an amazing responsibility to begin to come to terms with Karski's legacy and to shape his story into a performance.

The first two people I reached out to are the other two people who are part of this conversation. And that was within, I don't know, hours, days. David and I had collaborated previously on some work, particularly around a shared relationship to the great Studs Terkel, and David is obviously a performer I had admired. I had a sixth sense that something about Karski—his particular grace and humility and energy and spirit . . . I just thought of David right away, and called him up, and he was generous and interested right from the beginning. And Clark, as you know, Deborah, is a former student and longtime, trusted collaborator. The task seemed very daunting, just literally at a kind of biographical and dramaturgical level, to absorb the story quickly enough and to understand it responsibly. If I'm being honest, I didn't trust myself to do that, or to get it right in the time we had. And I wanted someone I trusted deeply to collaborate on that with.

And so, fortunately, both of them came on board. That first iteration you alluded to was developed as a one-off special event in Gaston Hall at Georgetown, with David performing as Karski in a staged reading with a group of students who played the rest of the ensemble. The conceit was the students were asking Karski questions as their professor and those questions became the engine through which we would flashback and witness episodes of Karski's life, and the students would then inhabit those roles. Our plan at that time was just to perform it once as part of the centennial. We had a few days of rehearsal for that staged reading. So that was my initial involvement.

DEBORAH: David, when I see you up there, I'm seeing Karski.

DAVID: We certainly hope so, since the piece is essentially a prism or lens through which to discover him. And thank you for your compliments. As Derek said, I got the call from him, which awakened a memory that I'd been carrying with me ever since seeing Jan Karski in Claude Lanzmann's documentary *Shoah*. I had walked around in a fog for days. I was stunned. For me, Karski's searing testimony was the centerpiece of the documentary. Several years later, while working in Canada, I met a man, who has since become a dear friend, who had left Poland around 1968, and one day when talking about the political history of

Poland, Jan Karski's name came up again. This was some time in the 1990s. So *Shoah* 1985 was first base. Canada the '90s, second. Derek's call, third base. And now here we are, all at home doing this. And what I've discovered in this "run around the bases" is that I have all along felt some connection with the man. Not a direct connection, but a connection to what he represented and what he did. Now I've come to appreciate him in much, much more depth having been a part of the development and collaboration and performed this piece for so long. So, to answer your question, it all started with Derek calling.

DEBORAH: You didn't have to say, "I'll think about it and get back to you tomorrow!"

DAVID: No, I didn't. I must have thought about it, but there was no doubt. It was only—"How is this going to happen?"

DEBORAH: I'll make one more comment—I'm sure many people have observed this—that there's a physical resemblance that is really striking. But one of the things I so appreciate is that— you got his accent down, but it's more comprehensible. I actually often had trouble understanding Jan Karski when I spoke with him because his accent was thick, and I have a hearing impairment. So, you know, for me, that was a problem. It's like, you get glasses and things become clearer. His words become clearer when you perform them.

DAVID: That's good to know because, as my Polish friend said, his accent is actually a little more eccentric, and a little different than a common Polish accent. It was probably a combination of the injuries to his jaw from being tortured by the Nazis. And, perhaps, even his learning so many languages as a young man. I don't know. But it is a very particular sound. And I suppose the older I get, the more I'll start to look like him.

DEBORAH: I know we'll come back and talk about how the play evolved and how the character evolved, but, Clark, first, your initiation into this?

CLARK: You know, I wish I'd been walking by the Karski statue at the same time as you, Deborah, because then you would have tapped me on the shoulder, and I would have known who this person was. Instead I went to Georgetown for four years and never bothered to interrogate that space, thinking of it as more of a novelty, something cute. Maybe something reverential, but never essential.

Derek didn't have to try hard to reach me. I was his former student and was working in theater and education in DC and, most importantly, was living rent free in his basement. The kindness of the Goldman family—all four of them. So, it was very easy for him to get a hold of me. He just needed to go down there. Little did I know that same little space would be where David also stayed for many weeks and where we would rehearse the piece as it exists today. It's quite a basement.

DEREK: Actually, I was in New York, I had to call you at my house. You took the call at my house. I remember the conversation, and I was not home. But Clark was.

DEBORAH: I didn't know that.

CLARK: Right, right. So, you know, as Derek is wont to do, he said, "There's a book on one of my shelves." And I had to go searching through these horribly messy bookshelves to find one biography. It was like the end of *Raiders of the Lost Ark*. But I found it, and I started to pore over his life.

Unlike Derek and David, I was faced with this question, this dilemma of not knowing. They both had knowledge through Holocaust theater, Holocaust education, watching

Shoah—I didn't have that. As a student, I conveniently internalized the history as an evil happening far, far away—and was maybe even taught that. I knew nothing about Allied inaction. And so, to open it, to crack it open, and to read E. Thomas Wood's biography on Karski, or to read Karski's own memoir, *Story of a Secret State*, to sit down and watch *Shoah* with Derek, as we did . . . I think that first week was really mind blowing for me. Particularly the clip of Karski breaking down in *Shoah*. It became this question, this looming question of how to theatricalize his inability to speak, that desire to not be on camera, that desire to wish so badly to not go back in his memory, as he says. And, yet, Karski always did for us, for future generations. That quickly became a real lodestar for all three of us. We jumped in, and I took over the dramaturgical and historical aspects of it and began to weave the pieces together.

And there's no coincidence, of course, that the play originated as a piece about a teacher and his students, because I was a student of Derek's, and we had lived in this liminal space of education, art, and advocacy. And Karski seemed to represent a perfect combination of all of those elements. Having witnessed and reported what he did, having dedicated his life to teaching and having married an artist in Pola Nirenska . . . it felt imperative to fit those pieces together. That's something that haunted all three of us, I think. In perpetuity, in all likelihood.

DEBORAH: And you all created it as a play based on Karski's words, right? Are all the words in the play and in the film his words?

CLARK: Almost entirely, through adaptations of either his memoir or biographies about Karski as well as oral histories and transcripts from the United States Holocaust Memorial Museum and the USC Shoah Foundation. Also, historical documents and footage at the Library of Congress. One of the incredible things about looking through the archives is that, you know, once Karski decides to speak about his experiences again in 1981 at the International Liberators Conference, after thirty-five years of self-imposed silence, we then found archives of Karski speaking every five to ten years until his death in 2000. And so you really get to witness the way he coached himself to talk about this, and how he learned to apply his life and trauma to the events of that particular time period. How he continued to talk about Holocaust denial and crimes against humanity through a lens that young people could receive and use.

DEBORAH: It's such a fascinating point. That in a way, you're continuing his work of reshaping the lessons of his life for not just new generations but for new generations of students. Do you want to say something about the course that you co-created?

DEREK: We wanted to think of the educational component as engaging with the relevance and immediacy of Karski's story and legacy today, and so the act of bearing witness was centralized at the very beginning. This goes back to the origin of the project in that 2014 presentation on Georgetown's campus, even the role of those remarkable initial students, who as cast members were part of that learning experience. In a sense the questions they were asking of Karski in that version were all of our questions and have animated the entire journey of developing this project over six years. The educational aspect was woven in already to the artistic work. It took Lanzmann asking Karski questions after decades of silence for his memories to pour forth, and it took us asking those questions to get toward the heart of this story. So that impulse to foreground how this story applies to and matters in the lives of young people today has been at the heart of the project from the beginning.

And then I think the journey has been to figure out how to do that theatrically in a way that isn't just didactic or pedantic or a lecture, which is not itself the most theatrically interesting thing. All of those stages were workshops and readings of a play in development. And it's only this version, the solo version that we shared fully in November of 2019 at the School of Foreign Service Centennial in Georgetown, and then, in January of 2020, in London as part of the seventy-fifth anniversary of the liberation of Auschwitz and Holocaust Remembrance Day. That's the beginning of the journey of the completed play.

Now, we've built out a course and curriculum, and we piloted it in the fall of 2020 as part of Georgetown's Just Communities program. This is a program emerging out of the joint realities of the pandemic and the reckonings around systemic racism and racial justice in our country, and the desire to engage in student-centered dialogue around these sets of critical issues. So the course was built in that context, and we call it Bearing Witness: The Legacy of Jan Karski Today. The Holocaust is a too little-known history by young people. And part of the work of this piece is to make people aware of that history. But I think even more than that, for us, it's about engendering dialogue in young people today about what they're bearing witness to, and what it means to carry on Karski's legacy of individual responsibility, of moral courage, of being good to your neighbor. Karski says: "Don't make distinctions." Clark and I created the course along with a brilliant educator named Ijeoma Njaka, who's been working with The Laboratory for Global Performance and Politics as our inclusive pedagogy specialist. The curriculum is designed to reach students in their own lives and to connect Karski's legacy with issues that they are passionate about. And we could not have been more moved by the depth with which our first students engaged with the course. How inspiring they were. Just extraordinary as a pilot group, many of whom now want to be "ambassadors" for the project going forward, and that has put wind in our sails in terms of our plans to scale this educational offering in conjunction with the film and with the play, so that we can bring many, many, many more students into those conversations, not only at Georgetown but hopefully around the world.

CLARK: The play began with young people. With students from Georgetown, and students from Poland, from Kraków, when we read the play in Warsaw. As the play gained a greater profile, we started to use professional actors. I felt something was lost, through no fault of the actors. There was a sense that the performance of not knowing was more important than the not knowing itself—the soul of what we all bear witness to, the things we see that we struggle to comprehend. So we put it to bed for a little while, humbled by how difficult the task was, and then returned with the idea of a one-person show that removed the device of students in order to engage the audience as the students. Now there's no affectation of learning. It's literal, it's communal in both the play and the film. And now, we're returning to our origin by creating the course and reapplying what we've created to bring young people back into the ensemble.

Students are hungry to be asked these questions. There are so many assumptions about what young people believe and think and don't want to deal with. And what's been fascinating about this project is that the play begins and ends with intentionally open-ended questions that students then use to talk about racial justice and allyship; the pandemic, the ignorance around science, the denial of science. They bring it to climate change and the ways in which we continue to ignore or are complicit in that great crime. They bring it to the challenges of creating productive discourse across ideologies and relationships and social media platforms. And so there is this sense of young people just wanting the chance to be asked those questions, to apply Karski's life to what they're seeing and what they're bearing witness to.

DEBORAH: There's something else that came to mind that's so relevant to today and what you both are saying—there's so much talk about patriotism. And Karski was a tremendous Polish patriot. He started working for the Polish Underground after they had been invaded by the Germans. The Jews were not a part of his initial purpose with the Underground. And then, when he was going to be sent to tell the Allies what was happening to the Poles, it was suggested that he also report on what was happening to the Jews. It was not a foregone conclusion that he would say, "Sure." Even those who asked him, I would guess, probably thought the chances he would say yes were slim. The fact that he agreed to do that is such a huge thing to get your head around. In the early parts of the play, we see that, for some reason, he didn't share the antisemitic assumptions that were prevalent at that time. When he was a kid and saw the Jewish kids getting persecuted, he stood up for them. That's such a fascinating side of his psychology, of this story. We think of it as a Holocaust story, whereas it really wasn't originally, from his point of view. He was doing a job for his country. And now there's so much discussion about what patriotism is. Are patriots the people who stormed the Capitol in January 2021? Are patriots those who call out their country for things that the country is doing that are not admirable?

DAVID: You touched on a couple of really potent, pivotal moments that we put into the piece. One is the scene when Karski's mother sends him outside and tells him to watch out for the kids throwing dead rats over the roof, tormenting young Jewish kids in the Sukkah where they pray. She tells him, "Go watch, like a good Catholic boy. If somebody comes, tell me, and I will take care of them." That moment, I think, is very significant. It informs another pivotal moment: his decision, years later, to meet with Jewish leaders in that nightmarish scene in "an old house on the outskirts of Warsaw," just before he goes to London to report to the Allied Nations. These moments reveal his innate empathic nature, which his mother had nurtured in him. As he said, "My Mother was very Catholic. Devotion. Respect for others. She was making us in her image." In that nightmarish scene in Warsaw, he agrees to bear witness on behalf of the Jewish people. I'm continually trying to find these handles to carry me forward into the psychology of the man. Those two moments are very, very significant to me.

And I think it's interesting to note what you said Deborah, that, initially, Karski wasn't aware of what was happening in the Warsaw Ghetto, which is extraordinary, that he wouldn't have known. That easily transfers to people today who don't really know what's going on at the border, what's going on in the halls of our government, what's really going on in the streets of our cities, what's going on with policymakers—people don't really know. They only know what they're being fed. Karski's journey represents the awakening of a conscience of a person. And that's what I hope for these students, that their conscience or consciousnesses, their awareness of what goes on in the world, is being awakened. And, through the vehicle of this performance, which is performed as direct address to them, we hope it respects their curiosity and hunger, which Clark mentioned. I have a kind of a crackpot theory about "curiosity" today . . .

We're assaulted with so many facts and opinions, and one could say we're being told how to form our own ideas. Basic curiosity is being dampened down by the technology we are slaves to. And so, in the classroom, when you awaken curiosity, I think that that awakens a vital part of learning, of being a student, being a citizen of the world. I think you're right, Clark. Had it been presented as a more traditional play, there would have been a veil that may have created an obstacle between a person's reaction and the material. This is a play that hinges on some very basic and vital questions we ask ourselves and each other. And to offer these questions, seeking real answers from the audience, is a very different neurology of performance.

DEREK: David's not just saying that abstractly. He has actually been able to connect with these students. And David has been so articulate about how that has moved and fueled him. And that's something you can't make up. There's a kind of intimate, vulnerable offering that these searching questions represent that was central for our team. We've been working on this story over the last six years of our history, the shift we processed when Obama was president to now—what stayed the same, what changed, what was exposed. We were constantly grappling, and the roles, I would say, of writer, director, performer are quite blurred. David is a true co-creator of the text of the piece, with the sensibility of living the man and playing that role. Obviously, when we made the solo play version and the film, it widened even more to an amazing core group of artists, but I would just say there's something about the fact that the play feels filled with questions and discoveries that we had ourselves about the world that we're living in now, through Karski. And we don't have the answers; we have the hard questions, which are intimately shared with students/audience members, who are then invited into thinking about them. Part of the beauty of this process is to witness students realize that within this extraordinary performance, which—on one level, they are very in awe of David's virtuosity—is coming from someone who is searching himself, who is looking to answer the same questions they're being asked. In most cases, they have better answers than we do. There's also a generational dynamic, even among the three of us, that I think has served the creation of the piece, and Clark is now in a generation that's not the generation of the students experiencing the piece. So we, in a way, have four generations going on, and I think that's powerful.

CLARK: And the students bring necessary diversity. We are three white guys writing about a fourth. But Karski's humility and allyship coats the entirety of the project's aspirations. And, Deborah, this mystifying question about patriotism is pinballing around in my head. Because Karski eschewed the label of "hero." He considered himself a failure regarding his mission, which is also part of his humility. There was no chauvinism or ego connected to what he was doing. And it seems to me that if I were to define patriotism, through Karski's lens, as I see it—and so many of these words mean nothing anymore because we use them so often in bad-faith arguments that they become charged by something else we can't control, words like "privilege" or "civility" or "patriotism," you don't know what they will mean to someone else who has a different media diet, upbringing, or identity—but I think that Karski recognized his own privilege within a dire situation, whether that's being Catholic, or working for the Underground, or being able to leave Poland for London and the United States. And he decides to do what's right, not what's right for him. Even years later, he could have stopped talking about it, he chose to be silent for some time, to protect himself. And yet, he returned. He continued to speak at the expense of his own mental health, of his wife's mental health, to continue to testify because it was the right thing to do on behalf of others, to continue to tell this story, especially in light of Holocaust denial in the world and in his home country, which he so loved and fought for. And so, to me, that's what makes Karski a patriot, if there is such a thing. He always did what was right, not what was right for him.

DEBORAH: And one of the reasons it's such an effective work of art is that you see Karski's evolution throughout. It's not like he has all the answers. And that point that you made, David, is so powerful and I'm now focused on it. He himself didn't know what was going on—in the camps and in the ghetto. And then having seen it, what did he choose to do with that, with that knowledge . . .

DEREK: And his extraordinary sense of failure, his sense of doubt and shame, which so defined him. One of the gifts we've had is developing this at Georgetown, even though none of us got to know Karski. Personally, I came to Georgetown a few years after he passed away. But in meeting and talking with so many people who did know him well, his former students and colleagues, that comes up over and over. His own expression of the failure he felt. That's what humanizes the journey. His own questioning and doubt. His lack of arriving at a place of anything that resembles not only victory but satisfaction. Something remained profoundly unfinished from his own perspective.

DEBORAH: There is one moment in the film that is unforgettable to me. When Karski meets with and reports to Supreme Court Justice Felix Frankfurter. Frankfurter's response is, "I don't believe you." And the Polish ambassador says, "But he's not lying." And Frankfurter says, "I didn't say he was lying. I said that I don't believe it. These are different things." That is an amazing thing to get your head around, especially these days, when so much is being disbelieved, so much is being questioned that we know is scientifically proven.

DAVID: Karski, in one of his later interviews, gives Frankfurter a bit of an out by saying he may not have been able to conceive of such a horror. And I believe in there, in the deep canyon of Karski's soul, or psyche, there is forgiveness. He forgives this man for not being able to conceive of something so horrific. That is such a rare thing. Especially today. What, you can't believe what is happening in the streets of Chicago? You can't believe what is happening down in El Paso? What do you mean, you can't believe that? There are pictures. There is reporting. What don't, or can't, you believe?! I think Karski was actually forgiving the fragile psyche of humanity for not being able to conceive of horrors that are inconceivable. And how then do you move forward with that knowledge? That is another one of those mysteries about this extraordinary man.

Yeah, in today's world of "alternate facts," how do you encourage the truth? How do you do it? How do you inspire a younger generation to go into deep exploration for the truth when they are being assaulted with so many lies? And how do we know what the truth is? It was the truth because, as Karski said, he saw it. How do we see things today? I believe the uncertainty of whether what we're seeing is true or not has a lot to do with how we participate in the world. Uncertainty and complacency have our shoelaces tied together. But when you come across a vital moment of awakening, as Karski did, what are you going to do with that? What are you going to do? What are you going to do with what you have just discovered?

DEREK: One of the most important lines for me in the piece, after going through this extraordinary journey, walking through the ghetto and the camp, all of that detail and all of the things he's bearing witness to and observing, he comes out of it and says, "All I can say is that I saw it, and it is the truth." There's no difficult word in that sentence, right? It's all three- to five-letter words. But in our current moment, that line has been such a visceral bedrock. How can you possibly say that this isn't what I have witnessed, that it is anything less than a truth that needs to be attended to? It's such a powerful line in 2020 and 2021, when, as you say, facts are contested at every turn.

CLARK: I do not share Karski's ability to forgive or, maybe better, resist judgment. I'm working on it. I certainly began more perplexed by Frankfurter. But, over time, I've grown angrier about Karski's interaction with Roosevelt. Because Roosevelt doesn't ask a single question about the Jewish problem, as Karski says of their meeting, and it's clear from 1938 on that his antisemitic and bigoted policies contributed to this disregard. Karski, twenty-nine years old, walks in, looks at this famous person in a position of power, who basically says, "Hello. You're a hero. Hope you come back. See you later." Karski presents that meeting in a very journalistic way. He's not condemning the president; he's presenting what happens exactly. But I find that to be even more soulshattering because Roosevelt could truly do something. Karski wasn't the first to discuss this with him. Yes, Roosevelt creates the War Refugee Board in 1944, which saved lives, but even its first director, John Pehle, called it "too little, too late."[1] Every day Roosevelt was making decisions about the war, including not to join until he had won his reelection, and until the United States had actually been attacked, which elevated the population's jingoism. So to not even deign to struggle with lying versus belief as Frankfurter did, to just dismiss someone's concern in that room and continue to go about ignoring through policy choices is something that really resonates with me right now—whether it's horrid policy choices around our health care system throughout this pandemic or our choice to uphold systemic racism throughout our justice system.

DEBORAH: But Roosevelt saw him! Churchill refused to.

CLARK: True, yes. Equally, equally frustrating. Yes, you're totally right.

DEBORAH: Roosevelt didn't do anything more than Churchill did, but something led him at least to meet him.

DEREK: That's one of the complexities of that scene, which is often prismatic for people. Karski is so insistent himself on these forensic descriptions of what happened. Never editorializing or evaluating or blaming. He leaves it for us to parse. I think that's a question—whether there were aspects of what Karski said that surfaced anything for Roosevelt. Or did he just reflect back and engage this young man in conversation. But there's a kind of depth of engagement, a kind of empathic focus that feels lacking from Roosevelt in that exchange. Even if there were understandably things that Roosevelt could not reveal to the young Karski, there is an almost tragic dimension of misconnection.

CLARK: And that word keeps coming up—empathic. There's a difference, I think, between a civil discourse and an empathic discourse. We always say, "We need civility in this room!" Well, there was plenty of civility in that room with Roosevelt, right? Karski walked in, bowed in reverence to this man, Roosevelt had his iconic cigarette out, welcoming him. It's all very pleasant, very civil, but people are dying, and no one's asking about it. It's insane! It's insane that we mistake civility for some kind of empathy. Civility often protects those in power from feeling empathy and taking action.

DEBORAH: So many thoughts are going around in my mind. That's one of the paradoxes of Karski. On one hand, the empathy that he clearly had an overabundance of, and yet, he often presented himself as a camera, a recording device. He would say, "It's not my job to tell anybody how to feel. It's not my job to feel." He used his remarkable photographic memory, which is astonishing to think about. But that's a huge paradox, which captures something about his power and the power of witness. That's another theme through all of this—the power of bearing witness.

I want to make one last comment about that moment of difference, the line between "I can't believe that" and "I don't believe it." It is this tiny little change with a world of difference! I think that's been part of the human condition forever. How do you know what people tell you is true? There are languages that have linguistic markers—we call them evidentials—that tell you how the speaker knows what they just said. In those languages, when someone says something, they can add these linguistic bits that tell you, "I know because I saw it." "I know because somebody told me," and so on. I wish English had them. Though if it did, we would probably misuse them! I think that's always been the case for human beings—the dilemma of deciding what to believe. But it's so much more extreme and challenging now, because of the ability to manipulate images. You know, you can say "I saw it," but what if what you saw isn't a real picture. A person was moved, was pasted into the picture, was taken out of the picture. It's an amplification of this dilemma of the human condition.

DEREK: Not to mention the failure of memory. There's that dimension.

DEBORAH: Yes. Yes. Exactly. Now I want to have you talk a little bit about the evolution of Karski through all these iterations and also your own personal evolution in living through it.

CLARK: It's a little bit of a carryover from our previous conversation, but I think it matters and is one of the evolutions of the piece. In my writerly brain, I have a resistance mechanism to the plainspoken truth. I want to flower things up with anecdotes and jokes. I want to add the things that made Karski such a unique professor to so many people. And one of the evolutions of the piece, I think, that I resisted, but Derek really advocated for, is the sparse, clinical use of language in the piece. It's very specific. It's very simple. It's very direct. Just as Karski reported. And I think that that's one of the writerly evolutions of the piece. We began on a trajectory taking large passages from different testimonials and anecdotes about Karski. And it became clear that this piece didn't need that. It needed to be direct. "All I can say, is that I saw it, and it is the truth." That is the ethos of the whole piece, as Derek said.

DEREK: There are a lot of things on the cutting room floor.

CLARK: There are. It really was like, "Okay, what is essential to the truth of Karski?" And what is essential to any moment in time that can be applied to Karski. And the simpler we were, the more I felt it popped with contemporary resonance.

DAVID: Well, it's interesting you say that, Clark, because this pristine authority of Karski's words, and the simple reporting of his history, makes it more direct and more confrontational, if you will. It asks us to confront the realities of which he speaks. It's a direct invitational to confrontation. Or at least an acknowledgment. What I have discovered, as a performer, as an actor doing this piece and being in the room with people who are experiencing it, is that it has made me very intolerant of extraneous talk in dramatic literature. And I will mention two people who, in terms of their verbiage are at complete extremes, and yet for me are the masters of the use of language to evoke ideas and feelings. Tom Stoppard and Harold Pinter. Having spent so much time thinking about, talking about, and performing this piece, I've found that I'm more and more impatient with material that is too self-conscious, or too expositional, too fluffy you could say, as we dance around what's really happening. I approach material—is this a story I want to hear? What am I going to learn from this story? Is this going to make me a little bit wiser, smarter? Is it going to open up my heart a little bit more? That's one of the things that has grown with me with this piece, and has informed me as a person, trying to find a way to cut through all the brambles out there and find common ground, a common place of safety and tolerance and acceptance in conversation. Because he did that in his way, Karski did. He served the message in a way that I think all artists try to do. Don't be the message; serve the message in whatever way you can. So that's what's been bubbling up with me over the last six years with this piece.

DEBORAH: Did your sense of who Karski was evolve? Or did the aspects of who he was that deeply moved you evolve?

DAVID: Yes, and they continue to. I'm more and more trying to somehow view the performance, the next time we do it, through his spirituality, his depth of faith. I feel that there is something quite telling in that aspect of the man. I believe it was the bedrock of how he could get through what he had to get through. And I also believe it predicated the way he would tell the story. His sense of duty, his humility, and his unshakable faith—all of those things—which to me are huge mountains to climb. A reservoir that I feel I'm just barely dipping my toes into. And also his sense of humor. People said he had a great sense of humor. I'd love to try to amplify that a little bit more. People loved to be around him.

DEBORAH: Maybe the humor showed itself more in private.

DEREK: That's some of what's on the cutting room floor. The charm is there in David's performance, and you have to be in a live audience to see the way that's being received. It probably doesn't come through from just reading the script. Of course, there's not a lot of humor, but what is there is very important. Because it's part of what disarms us to allow the audience as students to be moved and charmed and to care—whether that's a reference to Karski needing a "Manhattan," or how he had to learn many languages in Poland because he "never knew who would take us over." There's a sense of wit and irony, and a lack of self-seriousness, which may seem ironic given how serious a man he clearly was. But in terms of the actual relationship or rapport that David is building with the community, which is the audience and the students, I think that's deceptively important. That's the intimacy again. It's a strong fiber woven into Karski, with both tenacity and delicacy to it. That's the human element of feeling, as you're saying, David, that this is someone you like. The piece doesn't work if he's not someone you want to spend ninety-five minutes with.

In terms of your beautiful question, Deborah, I'm most struck by how the piece has evolved over the life of The Laboratory for Global Performance and Politics, which I co-founded in 2012 with Ambassador Cynthia Schneider. This piece was launched quite early in the official life of The Lab. And I feel this piece embodies the reasons why The Lab exists in the world, its mission of harnessing the power of performance to humanize politics. There's something about the way that it is a piece about questions, and dialogue, and a kind of open-endedness. That implies that in a world in which things are broken, and polarized, and where there are huge gulfs of belief, that there is some ability to shift by bearing witness differently. Maybe it's not a radical turn; maybe it's just an opening to a new way of thinking or understanding. There is something embedded in this piece, and in the power of Karski's story, that is, for me, deeply hopeful. The irony to this piece is that people say, "Oh, it sounds like a very dark, heavy piece." I experience it as hopeful because it is about claiming a sense that, especially for young people responding to these questions, Karski and David are suggesting paths forward by remembering this, this man and the legacy and the story, and embodying it in a way that invites others to speak into that memory, into that narrative. I feel more hopeful about the world. I don't find it despairing; it's given me an anchor. And the projects that I am looking for—like what David was saying about little patience for fluff—I feel like it's much clearer to me now somehow what projects would be worth doing or building on, even the kinds of things I'm covering in a curriculum or teaching. Somehow this story and this project have helped create a framework for myself around what's essential.

CLARK: Isn't it possible to feel both more hopeful and more deranged as this project has gone on? Because that's how I feel. I feel both. I understand what you're saying, Derek. But in order to have that anchor, you need to at least be looking around and feeling like, "Why do I need this darn thing always?" Those Zygielbojm questions, those small, simple questions—"Is there something I can do?" "What can I do that I'm not already doing?"—they've become a bit of a mantra for me because, of course, the figure of Szmul Zygielbojm is another evolution of the piece, right? He wasn't in the original staged reading in 2014. The truth is, I didn't understand what he was trying to say, and then we went to Warsaw. I started to understand more deeply the story of this Polish Jew in London waiting, watching, hearing, learning about his family dying, witnessing inaction and disinterest abroad. And I began to understand the profound effect that Zygielbojm's suicide had on Karski. They feel like two sides of the same coin. This one person who is so, so lost and unable to do anything besides taking his life in protest. And then another who keeps moving forward but, over a very long period of time, is able to finally say, "It haunts me now, and I want it to be so." There's this odd balancing act of seeing what goes on in the world and allowing yourself to be totally perplexed by our inability to learn any lessons, our inability to hold them, to teach, to listen. This is our reality. If I allow myself to be haunted by it, if I make those small choices, those little choices in life, that move toward what I think is a better future, is that the anchor I'm clinging to? I don't know.

DEBORAH: That's such a powerful point. In a way, Zygielbojm is someone who really saw it. He really saw it. And when you really see it, and you are not in a position to do anything about it, maybe that dramatizes our impulse to block it out. Now, that doesn't explain why Roosevelt should ignore it, because he could have done something, but what about those who felt they couldn't do anything?

I want to ask about this year. The pandemic came in the middle of all this. And I think people would love to know how you managed to make this film amidst a pandemic.

DEREK: Serendipity and happy accidents. We owe this to our collaborator and producer, Eva Anisko, who attended the performance in London. We've really only performed this piece theatrically a couple of times. It has not yet had a theatrical run. We had bookings in Edinburgh and Spoleto, Italy, and the McCarter Theater in Princeton, and it was going to go to Poland. That was all postponed. So, when we did perform it in London, Eva, a Polish

American and Georgetown alumnus who's an Emmy Award–winning documentary film producer, saw the piece. We met at the reception, and she was really moved by it, and she asked if we had a plan for doing anything with film. We exchanged information, and then the pandemic hit, and all of these plans and bookings were put on hold. We reached back out to Eva, and she worked miracles in the context of the pandemic to put a team together and get COVID approvals and find a studio in Brooklyn. Looking back, it really was a miracle that all of those pieces came together. She had collaborated with a brilliant director of photography, Jeff Hutchens, who became the co-director of the film with me, and, responding to the theater piece, he had a vision to shoot it in black and white in long, uninterrupted takes, an inspired vision that we all really believed in and connected to. And we got together for a week, six days of shooting, which is a very small amount of time to do what we did. And it feels like such a gift on so many levels.

This is still a theater piece. We want to have both out in the world. But the film does its own thing. It's a unique experience, a different viewing experience than the theater piece. And, of course, theater is just so ephemeral, even in the best of times, so there's something about knowing that there's a version of this work that exists. And we've barely shared it. That's the next step—figuring out where and how the film will move through the world. But it was a real blessing that Eva was able to pull together this brilliant team to do it.

DEBORAH: The film is astonishing. And as I said, having seen the play, I didn't expect to be rocked back by the film as much as I was. The use of light, the use of sound—it really is a work of art in its own way. David, what was it like doing it on a stage versus for a film?

DAVID: It's challenging to describe the communality of theater versus the individual reception of film. I can't wait to do it again with a live audience. I think the power of the piece really lies in its being live. Because there's something that happens in the room, with photons and electrons and people all being in the same space and strangers sharing this experience. We're all one, really, sharing something together. Film is a lot different. Not so much a communal activity anymore. But the film is now being used in the classroom. So that's good. It's a conduit from the two dimensional to the third or fourth, or fifth dimensional. I just hope we can get it back on its feet. Back in the presence of people.

DEREK: The other thing that the film provides that is more challenging with theater, of course, is that Karski is such an interior figure, and there's an access that the film team found that allowed David to master the subtlety and nuance of Karski. I knew that would happen intellectually, but I find, even when I now go back and look at the film, that I'm startled by how certain moments that are so subtle move me so deeply. A little swallow or an extra blink actually tells a whole story. And, of course, you're getting a version of that in an intimate theater experience, which is that it's never the same each night. But I do think there's something there that shows they really are companion pieces. To me, it's not an either/or thing. I think these both have a very important role to play. I don't have a preference. I feel like they're doing two really different things.

DEBORAH: I definitely felt that. Because, David, when you're doing it in the film, you are so close. And as a viewer, we get to see every nuance of facial expression. It feels so direct. You're speaking to us as Karski, and the film audience are the students engaging. You really feel that. On some level, I feel it's also altruistic for you to do it as a film. Having to perform the same scene over and over and the fragmentation of it compared to the theater—where you start at the beginning, get to build the emotional experience as you perform it—in a film you have to get yourself to that place, without having just done everything before. You've got to remember it. It just seems almost like an act of altruistic sacrifice, to do this piece in that format.

CLARK: It made me think a lot about Karski . . . never to conflate what Karski did with what David's doing. But, of course, having to go into a room and report the same thing over and over and over again, to report, to report, to report, right? To not change the way you're reporting, to not let the day's events or the audience change you, to have this take be exactly as precise as the next one, to try to find that space to be a true messenger on behalf of someone. To step into the shoes of another person and say, "This is what happened." What was unique about the film was watching David—who at times looked like a madman, I'll be honest—to watch David really step into Karski and have a deeper relationship to what it means to carry his message, to do the work of becoming his messenger.

DEBORAH: There might be a parallel. It was a sacrifice for Karski to do that, clearly. Because when he told it, he was back there. We're listening. We're where we are, but he isn't where we are. He's living through it again. And I think that was true for you, David.

CLARK: One other aspect I love about what we did with the film— so many movies depict violence in such ridiculous ways, so as not to believe them. And our team is not using the obvious tools of film to tell this story. It's a theatrical piece that's been infused with filmic qualities, and what I really dig is that we mostly use the tools that Karski had. He had storytelling. He had his memory. We can't see what happened; we're being asked to believe him. And I think in a way that's a subversive take on what it means to depict the Holocaust in film. You're being challenged to imagine it yourself.

DEREK: A man, a desk, and two chairs.

CLARK: Right? That's it.

DEREK: I do find I return to the conditions of a class, of any class-room, anywhere. There's a teacher and others who've come into the room. A desk and chairs. There's a Polish theater tradition that this harkens back to, which is a very spare, elemental theatricality. The legacy of Tadeusz Kantor and his hugely influential work *Dead Class*, which takes place in a simple classroom. And one of the things that really attracted us to Jeff as a collaborator was that he understood that and was building a kind of cinematic language to support and amplify that rather than trying to compete with it or transform it into something completely different.

DEBORAH: I want to ask each of you if you wanted to say something about how you feel you're a different person now than you were before all this, but it's up to you guys if you want to answer that.

DAVID: I feel much fuller. You know, when you meet somebody like Karski, who has been through what he went through, and then leads such an exemplary life and a life of such complexity and mystery and grace . . . that's a gift. I feel like I have actually been gifted. I've been given in my lifetime a gift to cross the path of this man. It's been really very special.

CLARK: I can't say it better than that.

DAVID: And to find you two guys to do it with.

DEREK: This is true. It's an amazing piece of this. In the best sense of what being humbled is by a project or a process . . . I feel humbled in the face of something so powerful and mysterious and enormous. To keep alive this legacy and these questions, and to be able through that to be doing it with real love and friend-ship in collaboration. The sort of depth of trust we've found in each other through our own failings, of getting it wrong, of trying this version in the middle of the night. "I think it's this! Maybe the whole play is about this crazy man who comes in with a cart at the beginning with all of his belongings. And he's speaking in tongues!" That was an actual version on the table for a few days.

To work on hard, difficult things in a space of love and trust and to then be able to share that and have that widen out to others—that's a real once-in-a-lifetime gift.

DEBORAH: I want to thank all three of you for the gift of this cre-ation, and maybe it's chutzpah, but I also want to say thank you on the part of all the people who are going to see it, who have seen it and will see it. Because what you've created is so meaningful, so deep, doing something that couldn't be done any other way. And I think your love for each other is part of what gives this its soul. So, thank you.

Note

1. *Holocaust Encyclopedia*, s.v. "The War Refugee Board," accessed July 11, 2021, https://encyclopedia.ushmm.org/content/en/article/the-war -refugee-board.

DO SOMETHING, ANYTHING

Aminatta Forna

Do we have a duty, a responsibility, as individuals ... to do something, anything?

And then:

"Great crimes start with little things."

These are lines spoken in the closing scene of *Remember This*, authored by Derek Goldman with Clark Young, which tells of the Polish emissary Jan Karski's mission to America to warn Franklin Roosevelt of Nazi crimes against the Jews then taking place in his country. Against the odds of capture and death, Karski successfully escaped first Poland then mainland Europe, to Britain, where he failed in his attempt to reach Churchill. Finally, he arrived in America where he was received by and delivered his message to Roosevelt. Through the lens of history, we know that the slaughter of six million was never stopped.

When I was a child growing up in Sierra Leone, my father, Mohamed Forna, was a political activist. Before that he was a doctor and then a member of parliament and a cabinet minister. My father's political career did not last long, just a few years. He spent much of the rest of his life as a political prisoner because he had asked himself the same question that is posed at the beginning—and repeated at the end—of the play: "Do we have a duty, a responsibility, as individuals to do something?" And he had answered his own question. Yes, we do.

In 1974 my parents gave me an autograph book for Christmas. It was purple and had three stars on the front. That vacation I went around collecting autographs from various members of the family. My father had been home for Christmas that year, in between arrests by the security police. They came for him again the next summer and that was the last we would see of him. Years later and long after the book fell apart, I held onto the fading paper upon which my father had written these words: "Honor and shame in no condition lie. Act well your part, for there the honor lies." I was ten years old. Whatever I understood those words to mean at the time, their resonance has only grown greater the more I see of the world and of the actions and the inaction of men and women.

By the time of my father's death, Sierra Leone had moved from a nascent democracy to a one-party state to a fully fledged dictatorship. The man who had ordered his death was our president. Sixteen years after my father's death, the country would tip into a war that bore witness to countless deaths, maimings, rapes, and kidnaps. For many people in the world, the first they came to hear of our country was through news reports, which bordered on the frankly salacious, of the atrocities perpetrated upon civilians by rebel soldiers wearing women's wigs, of drug addicted child soldiers, and of amputees. It shocked me whenever anyone made any of those particular associations with the name of our country because that was not the Sierra Leone I knew.

When the war began, I was working as a journalist. At the same time as the Sierra Leone civil conflict was taking place, another conflict was brewing in Europe where the breakup of Yugoslavia had begun with dreadful consequences. You couldn't, or at least *I* couldn't, help but notice the difference in the ways in which the two wars were reported. The Yugoslav wars were reported in forensic detail, both politically and militarily.

This was less true in the case of Sierra Leone. The atrocities were covered, but otherwise the war was reported devoid of political context, described as a "tribal" conflict (it wasn't, although the Yugoslav war was the product of nationalism and ethnic divisions). Most of the coverage occurred in 1997 when Freetown came under attack and Western embassies decided to evacuate their personnel. My stepmother managed to escape at that time, accompanied by her husband, and would spend the next year and a half living with me and my husband in London. These were the days before social media, and news of the war, once the Westerners were safe, was scant. I remember how my stepmother was the first person I knew who heard the news of Princess Diana's death in a car crash in the early hours of August 31, 1997, because she was still awake, monitoring the late-night news for any reports on the situation in Sierra Leone. That year I began to formulate the idea for a book, one that I would eventually publish as a memoir, *The Devil That Danced on the Water.*

The events that led to the killing of my father had been marked by silence for more than two decades. The subject was never discussed openly, much less written about. And when the family talked about it among ourselves, we did so out of the hearing of others. We lived in a police state, where spies abounded and talk could land you in trouble. Still, I had witnessed a few key events and knew some facts. My father had resigned his ministerial position in protest to the then prime minister's corruption. Amnesty International had declared him a prisoner of conscience. I remembered visits from Amnesty representatives much as I remembered visits from the plainclothes police—except that the Amnesty people didn't go through our belongings and upend furniture.

The morning of September 12, 1970, I accompanied my stepmother to the residence of the British High Commission when she went to inform the high commissioner that my father planned to resign. It was my brother's birthday, and a party was being planned. My stepmother had fetched me from my bed. I suppose by leaving the house with a young child, she hoped to avert the suspicions of the guards and anyone else who might be watching. I was six years old. Later, when I was a teenager, I came to know that my father had made the reasons for his resignation public, although I did not know that his resignation letter had been carried in full by several newspapers.

In 2000, after the second invasion of Freetown, when the country was picking itself up out of the dust and destruction, I was back, taking part in the recovery effort and talking to anyone who remembered my father and the events of the 1970s. Over and over, people mentioned the resignation letter. A few people could even quote lines from it. Eventually I met a man, the editor of a newspaper, who was able to provide me with a copy.

The letter detailed a devastating list of allegations and assertions. My father accused the prime minister of corruption, of politically motivated violence toward the media and the opposition, and of megalomaniac behavior. In reference to a particular instance, a demand by the prime minister that the national anthem be played at a public appearance, something reserved for the governor general, he wrote: "This display of infantile vanity may appear trivial, but to me with a trained medical mind, they are the manifestations of a megalomaniac syndrome . . . This coupled with an insatiable thirst for power can only spell disaster to this country." Finally, he accused the president of planning to establish a dictatorship.

Soon after my father resigned, he was arrested and imprisoned. The new political party he had helped to found was outlawed, and he spent the next three years in prison. By the time of his release, all the key elements of a totalitarian state were in place. The prime minister had declared the country a republic and named himself president; the media was censored and brought under state control; the chief of police had fled into exile; the army had been emasculated and the head of the army killed; and the State House was guarded by armed militias loyal only to the president.

I remember my conversation with the newspaper man. I had said, "But my father had warned of this, exactly this. Why didn't anyone do anything? Why didn't they listen?" And he had answered that he thought most people in the country had not understood what my father meant. Democracy was too new; we had only become an independent nation a decade before. Those things my father described were unfamiliar. Of course, the editor himself had understood, that's why he had run the letter and why he had held onto it for so many years. He was one of a few educated people who grasped precisely the significance of events.

Some months later I went to interview a professor and his wife. He had been teaching at the university at the time of my father's resignation and subsequent arrest. I questioned them patiently, urged them to remember, which they did pretty well. Then I asked what they had done when they heard the news of the detentions. The interview took a turn. What do you mean? After the arrests and the imprisonments, I said, what did you do? They didn't understand. What was I asking them? I pressed on, making myself clearer. I was asking them because they had been members of the intelligentsia. What was the talk on campus, for example? Were there efforts to protest or to organize? Petitions? Letters to newspapers?

The couple had a daughter, a lawyer, who was my age and was sitting at a table in the same room, working. She had paused and was listening. I continued to ask questions, politely but persistently; her parents elided. Finally, she brought her hand down on the table, causing us all to turn around. She's asking you what you *did*? she said. After the arrests what did you *do*? Of course, by then we knew the answer. They had done nothing.

We became friends, that woman and I. And she has talked to me of her shame at her parents' inaction. She told me that later she had confronted her father and he had replied, "I had children. What could I do?" And I thought about his reply and knew my father would have said, "I have children. I must do something."

Around the same time, I met a woman from Argentina and, in the course of becoming friends, told her parts of my history. In return she told me a story of her own. She had grown up during the Dirty War in Argentina, when all dissent was crushed, when anyone with suspected left-wing sympathies was snatched from their home, from their workplace, or on the street; held in secret locations and tortured; thrown still alive out of helicopters and into the sea or tossed into a mass grave. Those people eventually became known by the name "the Disappeared." Years later it would come to light that children had been born to some of the women prisoners, and that those children were taken away and adopted into high-ranking military families. My friend's father had been an academic at the university. She described how his career had bloomed in those years. And how, once, he had warned her against involvement with a particular boy, one whose family were later disappeared. She never knew whether her father knew anything specific about the case or if he just didn't want her socializing with people who were politically active. Later on, as an adult, she was rankled by her father's success. Everyone who stood up to the injustices taking place paid some sort of price, perhaps losing a promotion or, worse, being forced into exile or even imprisoned, she told me. I looked at my father and at his great success, and I thought, how can it be so? How can it be so?

In *The Memory of Love*, a novel, I created a character, a man who didn't feel he had a duty to "do something, anything" or was simply too cowardly or too self-interested to act. Before he knew it, the moment for action had passed. Later he was unable to save his daughter from the consequences of living in a damaged country, one in which the rule of law had been overturned.

In my life I have spoken to a great many people who did nothing. My experience is that they will insist they never knew. Even when the killing started, they never knew. Even when thousands were killed—they never knew.

Again, lines from *Remember This*: "When Churchill speaks to Parliament in 1946, he says that he had no idea of the scale of these horrible massacres which had occurred, the millions and millions that had been slaughtered. That it dawned on him gradually after the war was over."

Roosevelt listened to Karski for a while, changed the subject, and sent him away. "Human beings have infinite capacity to ignore things that are not convenient."

On the eve of his execution, my father wrote a second letter. The president had issued him paper and a pen with which to write a letter, one in which he might plead for clemency. My father would have known this was a ruse to allow him to abase himself and then to kill him anyway. And so he wrote a letter to the nation, which was later smuggled out of the prison. The letter was kept hidden for twenty-five years; even my family did not know of its existence. The widow of the man who carried it on his person and through the prison gates found it upon his death and sent it to a newspaper. It was 2000. The regime that had killed my father had been overthrown eight years earlier. The war was coming to an end, with tens of thousands dead or displaced. My father seemed to speak from the grave. In the letter he had warned, again, of the end of the rule of law, of war. And he said: Let history be my judge. Suddenly, and even before the war was officially over, which it would be two years later, people had the answer to the question they had been asking themselves—How did this happen? And now they learned that some people had known it could. And that the people who might have changed the course of events had done nothing.

Today alarms are being sounded across America—by artists, writers, activists, and, most of all, by those who have experienced the rise of authoritarianism elsewhere. This is happening while we still have time to "do something, anything." If the worst happens, will those who did nothing say "I never knew"?

A LIFE IN SERVICE

THE INSPIRATION OF JAN KARSKI

Stuart Eizenstat

It is especially timely for the play and the movie *Remember This* to honor the memory and remember the lessons of Jan Karski. This is a troubling time, with a rising tide of hatred against people of color and increasing antisemitism as well as appalling declines in knowledge about the Holocaust and its contemporary lessons, particularly among young people, as more and more of the 330,000 survivors and eyewitnesses of the Holocaust are leaving us. It is also a time of genocides and potential genocides around the world. If we are to take seriously the pledge "Never again," we must apply the lessons of Jan Karski and acknowledge the importance of Holocaust education to meet our contemporary challenges. Karski's courage was certainly an inspiration for my work during the Carter, Clinton, and Obama administrations on Holocaust remembrance and justice.

Growing up in Atlanta, Georgia, I never met a Holocaust survivor; and despite having a father and two uncles who were in military service in World War II, the Holocaust was never a subject of discussion. In 1968 Arthur Morse published *While Six Million Died*, based upon newly declassified records of the Roosevelt administration. The book shockingly described what Roosevelt knew about the genocide of the Jews and how he failed to act. Morse was my colleague on Hubert Humphrey's presidential campaign, and his revelations included a description of Jan Karski's courageous but unsuccessful attempt in 1943 to rouse Allied leaders to action against the Holocaust. Karski met with President Roosevelt, who listened impassively, and with Supreme Court Justice Felix Frankfurter, who told Karski he chose not to believe him. This book, and the description of what Karski had witnessed firsthand in Nazi-occupied Poland, changed my life and committed me to a course of pursuing justice for Holocaust survivors and sustaining the memory of those who perished.

There was nothing inevitable about the Holocaust, nor is there about genocides around the world today. In fact, Roosevelt's and Frankfurter's indifference to the news of the plight of the Jews of Europe, brought directly to them by Karski, fit a pattern.

- At the Evian conference in July 1938, called by President Roosevelt to deal with the plight of German Jewish refugees, Roosevelt sent low-level representatives and failed to take the lead in lifting rigid immigration quotas while the State Department did all it could to restrict immigration.
- In May 1939 the SS *St. Louis*, carrying more than nine hundred German Jews, sat for days outside Miami and was not allowed to land.
- No sanctions were imposed on Germany before the United States finally entered the war.
- As Karski documented from his own visit, President Roosevelt had substantial evidence about the growing dimensions of the Holocaust but failed to act. Because of the high levels of antisemitism in America, Roosevelt did not want to make World War II seem like a war for the Jews. Karski's revelations helped lead to the creation of the War Refugee Board chaired by Treasury Secretary Henry Morgenthau, which saved hundreds of thousands of Jews in 1944–45. But so many more could have been saved if Roosevelt had acted upon Karski's shocking disclosures.

- Arthur Hays Sulzberger, publisher of the *New York Times*, gave his editors instructions to bury stories of the Holocaust, concerned that his paper would be viewed as a Jewish newspaper.
- The American Jewish leadership, with whom Karski also met, did not do all they should have to pressure Roosevelt to act more urgently, as they were also afraid of raising antisemitic sentiment.

All of this meant that Hitler received a clear signal, and said so publicly, that the world did not care about protecting the Jews, and he had a free hand to commit the worst genocide in world history.

In the immediate postwar period, Nazi atrocities were revealed with the liberation of death camps, which were filmed at the insistence of Supreme Allied Commander Dwight D. Eisenhower. While Americans were shocked by newsreels of the death camps, the staggering dimensions of the Shoah were not understood, and the Holocaust was quickly given a backseat, as the focus of the United States and the West shifted to the Cold War against the Soviet Union. This was evident in a number of ways:

- There was little demand for justice beyond the Nuremberg trials, which represented a tiny fraction of the Nazi perpetrators.
- Jews trying to reclaim their confiscated homes in Poland and Lithuania were killed, and postwar property restitution laws in countries such as France, Austria, and the Netherlands were inadequate.
- Many Jews lived in squalid displaced persons camps after the war. General George Patton, whose forces liberated concentration camps, ordered guards to monitor survivors as if they were inmates in prison. President Truman's representative on refugees, Earl Harrison, wrote a scathing report after visiting the displaced persons camps: "As matters

now stand, we appear to be treating the Jews as the Nazis treated them, except we do not exterminate them. They are in concentration camps in large numbers under our military guard instead of SS troops. One is left to wonder whether the Germans seeing this are not supposing that we are following or are at least condoning Nazi policy."[1]

- Great Britain kept fifty-two thousand survivors trying to reach Palestine in squalid camps in Cyprus, some up to five years.

- Elie Wiesel had difficulty finding a publisher for his book, *Night*, finally published in English in 1960. The same year Rabbi Irving Greenberg was denied the opportunity to teach a course on the Holocaust at Yeshiva University because it was not considered a proper topic for academic study.

But the monstrous dimensions of the Holocaust could not be hidden forever. The 1961 trial in Jerusalem of Adolf Eichmann, a top Nazi murderer dramatically taken by Israelis from his hiding place in Argentina, put a human face on the genocide of the Jews when it was broadcast to the world on television. Following Elie Wiesel's and Arthur Morse's books, a whole genre of books, movies, and documentaries came out, including Claude Lanzmann's classic nine-hour documentary, *Shoah*, and, later, *The Karski Report*, based on interviews of Jan Karski by Lanzmann from *Shoah*.

In addition, the Holocaust created, for the first time in the history of warfare, a legal process by which a country that had abused and murdered civilians—both its own and those of the countries it occupied—agreed to compensate survivors. On September 27, 1951, the first postwar West German chancellor, Konrad Adenauer, broke Germany's official silence and accepted responsibility, proclaiming that "unspeakable crimes" had been "committed in the name of the German people" and calling for "moral and material indemnity."[2]

One month after Adenauer's speech, Dr. Nahum Goldmann, president of the World Jewish Congress, convened a meeting in

New York of twenty-three major Jewish organizations, creating the Conference on Jewish Material Claims against Germany. Beginning in The Hague in March 1952, negotiations commenced between Germany and Israel, and parallel negotiations began between the German government and the Claims Conference, which were highly controversial both in Israel and in Germany.

In a historic agreement in Luxembourg on September 10, 1952, the Claims Conference and the West German government signed two protocols. One called for German laws that would compensate Nazi victims directly. The second protocol provided the Claims Conference with 450 million deutsche marks for the relief, rehabilitation, and resettlement of survivors. The history of Claims Conference negotiations with Germany over the decades has been to expand the number of Holocaust survivors eligible for payment through a variety of programs and to increase the amount paid to them through pensions, home care, and social services—almost all based upon need. Germany has now paid over $80 billion since the 1950s, and almost all of the major programs the Claims Conference negotiated with Germany have gone only to survivors in economic need. Even today there are approximately 350,000 Holocaust survivors around the world, of whom at least 50 percent are poor or near poor. More than half of these 350,000 survivors receive some form of payment from the German government.

The Holocaust was not only the greatest genocide in history; it was the greatest theft in history.

After the collapse of communism, Edgar Bronfman, president of the World Jewish Congress and the World Jewish Restitution Organization, met with President Bill Clinton to urge that a special envoy be appointed to encourage the newly democratic countries in central and eastern Europe to return communal property—synagogues, schools, community centers, even cemeteries—to the shattered Jewish communities seeking to rebuild after the twin tragedies of the Holocaust and communism. I became that special envoy, taking on a dual role while I was US ambassador to the European Union, and throughout my other senior positions in the Clinton administration at the Commerce, State, and Treasury departments.

In the midst of this work, I read a 1994 article in the *Wall Street Journal* about dormant Swiss bank accounts, opened by Jews seeking to avoid the Nazi seizure of their assets. These accounts were never returned to their rightful owners and were instead taken into the profits of the banks. In 1996 a committee, chaired by former chairman of the Federal Reserve bank Paul Volcker, was created to conduct an audit of the wartime Swiss bank accounts. Three years later the Volcker committee issued its report, finding that some 54,000 accounts had probable or possible Jewish owners, and over 20,000 almost certainly did. Ultimately, the Swiss banks agreed to a staggering settlement of class action suits I helped mediate, with the crucial involvement of US district court judge Edward Korman, for $1.25 billion. The Swiss bank case led to additional class action cases against German and Austrian slave labor companies, European insurance companies that never paid for life insurance policies, and the return of Jewish communal and private property, which I mediated. I also negotiated the forty-two-nation Washington Principles on Nazi-Confiscated Art, which, although voluntary, has profoundly changed the art world and led to the restitution and compensation of thousands of art works, books, and cultural and religious items. Still, it is only a small fraction of what the Nazis looted.

Belated justice for Holocaust survivors and the families of victims in the form of monetary and material compensation are not the most lasting lessons coming out of the tragedy. Holocaust education is now more critical than ever, both to remember the past and to learn the lessons of what happens when intolerance goes unchecked, when decent people fail to act in the face of injustice, whether based upon religion, ethnicity, race, or gender.

During the initial postwar years, the Claims Conference was fundamental in providing critical funding for Yad Vashem, the YIVO Institute for Jewish Research, the Mémorial de la Shoah in Paris, and the Wiener Holocaust Library in London. At its peak a few years ago, the Claims Conference was the largest funder of Holocaust education. But the fund has dwindled at the very time Holocaust awareness has dramatically dropped.

In a major recent survey, 48 percent of American millennials and Generation Z could not name a single one of the more than forty thousand concentration camps or ghettos; 56 percent were unable to identify Auschwitz; and 63 percent did not know that six million Jews were killed. Remarkably, 11 percent believed Jews caused the Holocaust. Roughly half have seen Holocaust denial or distortion posted on their social media platforms. However, the bright spot is that 64 percent felt that Holocaust education should be compulsory in their schools, and 80 percent believed it was important to learn about the Holocaust.[3]

There is progress. In 2020 the US Congress passed the Never Again Education Act to provide $10 million to promote Holocaust education through grants provided by the US Holocaust Memorial Museum. In January 2021 the German government agreed to provide the Claims Conference with over 50 million euros starting in 2020, over the next several years.

Has the Holocaust taught the world anything? Are we any better for the lessons it should have given us? Applying these lessons to the human rights violations ongoing today would be the most faithful commemoration of Jan Karski's legacy.

We have come far, as the world has developed a set of international instruments that have the potential of incorporating the lessons of the Holocaust and Jan Karski's bravery. But we have a long way to go. The Universal Declaration of Human Rights in 1948 adopted a nonbinding UN resolution that still remains a landmark. Since then there have been numerous international agreements such as the

- Genocide Convention;
- International Covenant on Economic, Social, and Cultural Rights;

- International Covenant on Civil and Political Rights;
- International Convention on the Elimination of All Forms of Racial Discrimination;
- Convention on the Elimination of all Forms of Discrimination against Women;
- Convention on the Rights of the Child; and
- Convention against Torture.

In the early 1950s the Council of Europe adopted the European Convention of Human Rights as a direct result of the Holocaust, establishing the first court to allow individuals to sue states that violate their rights. This is the European Court of Human Rights, which remains active to this day.

The International Court of Justice in The Hague was created in 1945 to be the principal civil court of the United Nations and hear disputes between countries. In 2020, in a recent case brought by Gambia against Myanmar, the court issued a provisional decision aimed at protecting the Rohingya from further persecution under the Convention on the Prevention of Genocide.

Moreover, international criminal law, and the institutions designed to enforce it, have evolved. This process began with the Nuremberg tribunal to try Nazi war criminals. In 1993 the UN Security Council established the International Criminal Tribunal for the former Yugoslavia, and several of the worst Serbian human rights offenders were tried and convicted, including Serb general Ratko Mladić. In 1994 the International Criminal Court for Rwanda was established following the Rwandan genocide. And in 2002 the International Criminal Court came into being, to which now over 120 nations (not including the United States) are parties. Radovan Karadžić, president of the Republic of Serbia, was convicted by the court, and forty-five world leaders, including Libya's Muammar Gaddafi, have been indicted by the court.

There are other institutions today that did not exist during the Holocaust. Human rights nongovernmental institutions such as Human Rights Watch, Doctors without Borders, Hebrew Immigration Aid Society, and Amnesty International highlight acts of genocide and war crimes. The US Holocaust Memorial Museum's Center for the Prevention of Genocide, to which I belong, thoroughly researches and works with members of the US government to highlight areas where genocide is occurring or where it is at risk of happening. The Auschwitz Institute for the Prevention of Genocide and Mass Atrocities has one of the largest education and training programs around the world. I chair the Defiant Requiem Foundation, which has performed more than fifty concert-dramas in the United States, Europe, and Israel to dramatize the power of cultural resistance through the arts and music.

The internet and aggressive journalists bring war crimes and acts of genocide directly into our homes to stir our consciences, something not possible during the Holocaust.

For all its limitations, the United Nations, operating under a UN Security Council Resolution since 1999, has numerous peacekeeping missions to protect civilians, providing some measure of protection Jews never had during the Holocaust.

The limitations of international law are all too painful. A critical factor is the willingness of the president of the United States (along with the Congress) to make human rights a key part of American foreign policy and to enlist our allies in Europe to do the same. I am proud that Jimmy Carter, whom I served on his White House staff, was the first to do so, and I believe President Joe Biden will put human rights back into a central role in his foreign policy. Of course, all presidents have to carefully balance America's interests against human rights concerns, as in dealing with China. But making human rights at least a significant part of foreign policy can help advance its cause and protect vulnerable people from genocide. The Holocaust has been a stimulant in beginning to build a world in which human rights violations and genocide gain greater opprobrium.

The most meaningful way to commemorate Jan Karski's bravery is to pledge ourselves and to urge our governments to remember the lessons of the Holocaust and to take effective action against hate, antisemitism, human rights violations, and genocide wherever and whenever they occur.

Notes

1. Earl G. Harrison, *Treatment of Displaced Jews,* 29 September 1945, Albert Hutler Collection of Articles and US Military Records Relating to Displaced Persons in Postwar Europe, RG-19.024.01, US Holocaust Memorial Museum, Washington, DC. President Truman to General Dwight D. Eisenhower, 31 August 1945, White House News Release, US Holocaust Memorial Museum, Washington, DC, https://www.ushmm.org/exhibition/displaced -persons/resourc2.htm.

2. Lily Gardner Feldman, *The Special Relationship between West Germany and Israel* (London: George Allen & Unwin, 1984), 40.

3. Conference on Jewish Material Claims against Germany, "U.S. Millennial Holocaust Knowledge and Awareness Survey," accessed on March 6, 2021, http://www.claimscon.org/millennial-study/.

BEARING WITNESS AND SPEAKING TRUTH TO POWER

A CONVERSATION

Azar Nafisi
and
Cynthia Schneider

CYNTHIA: Our conversation will be part of a volume about Jan Karski and the play *Remember This: The Lesson of Jan Karski*, produced by The Laboratory for Global Performance and Politics, which I co-founded at Georgetown University. It is such a pleasure to be able to have this conversation with you, Azar, as a continuation of your collaboration with The Lab, which has been such an honor for us.

Jan Karski bore witness to the horrors of the Holocaust. Yet, when Karski brought his testimony to the White House about what he saw in the Warsaw Ghetto and the transit camp to Belzec, President Roosevelt did not act on this information, or on Karski's urgent message that all the Jews in Poland risked extermination if the Allies did not take action quickly.

Instead, President Roosevelt assured Jan Karski that the Allies would win the war, and when they did, they would punish the wrongdoers and criminals. Roosevelt had his long-term strategic goal to win the war. This is realpolitik: you have a goal, you pursue the goal, without a particular focus on the human cost along the way.

But I wonder how this approach looks through the lens of the twenty-first century, when through social media we can see everyone's lives all over the world. Might Roosevelt have responded differently if the whole world had seen what Karski witnessed? Maybe not, but perhaps it's time to reevaluate realpolitik and to consider whether it isn't in a country's strategic interest to consider the human impact of policies. And, of course, artists are the ones who tell us what those human costs are.

What has been the relationship in Iran between its culture and voices of creativity and the regime?

AZAR: In Iran in a very ironic way, the regime understands how dangerous individual rights and human rights are to its existence, and it learned how important culture is to the Iranian people and their identity. The Iranian state eliminates the people who are most threatening to its rule. They target those at the forefront of the struggle: women, minorities, and those who are working in culture. They arrest them, they torture them, they kill them.

I was born in a culture where, before I learned how to read and write, I knew poems by heart from our classical poets; where people in traditional coffee shops have oral readings and perform our epic poet Ferdowsi's stories (early eleventh century).

When the current Islamic regime came to power, they brought down all the statues of the shah and his father, and they changed the name of the streets wherever the shah's name was, or his father's. Then they wanted to tear down the statue of Ferdowsi because his epic is about pre-Islamic Iranian mythology and histories, and they wanted to forbid anything pre-Islamic. They planned to change the names of the street honoring the poet Omar Khayyam (1048–1131) because he was agnostic. They couldn't do it.

People tolerated bringing down the statue of the shah, but they would not tolerate tearing down the statue of a poet. Now, forty years later, it is the regime that has to pay respect to the poets it was trying to obliterate. And that is a good lesson for me.

I always remember Vladimir Nabokov saying, "Governments come and go, only the trace of genius remains."[1] I wish our policymakers understood this. All they have to do is to go to history to see that governments do indeed come and go. And we still are talking about Homer.

CYNTHIA: Absolutely. I have a chapter in my book that is called "Extremists and Authoritarians Get Why Culture Matters: Why Don't We?" From a negative perspective, authoritarians and extremists understand the power of culture. And so they want to obliterate it, to achieve their goal of shaping history into what they wanted it to be. Whether it's the Iranian government, or the Khmer Rouge, or Hitler, they all do the same thing. They recognize the power of culture to move people. Ironically, the forces of good, the forces of more open, free societies do not recognize that power as much.

AZAR: Yes, you're right. I always think of the case of Salman Rushdie. Here's a man whose only weapon is his pen, his writing. He doesn't have any other power in the world. And who is his opposition? Ayatollah Khomeini, who has the military, the weapons, the Revolutionary Guards, and all sorts of means to impose oppression. Yet, Khomeini is so scared of Salman Rushdie that he gives a fatwa for Rushdie to be killed.

I always imagine how much power must one writer have. To think that his being alive is dangerous to the health of a whole totalitarian society. So what you said about your authoritarians recognizing their enemies is so true.

CYNTHIA: Picking up on this theme of the importance of writers and artists, you have been able to look at the United States in such an interesting way in your book *The Republic of Imagination* and to see the character of the United States through three writers. That's something I think that observers from the outside tend to do more than Americans.

Do you think there is something particular about America that we don't tend to embrace our creative culture as part of our identity? I sometimes wonder, is it because those creative voices are the ones who speak truth to power?

AZAR: Talking truth to power is one of the greatest dangers to the totalitarian mindsets, and totalitarian mindsets are everywhere, including in democracies. This is part of the reason why I'm writing my next book, which is titled *Reading Dangerously*.

The role of fiction, the role of all great art and literature, has always been speaking truth to power, going after truth. And once you reveal the truth, then you are responsible. Not only is the writer responsible but also the readers and the audience. People who pay attention to those great works of art and literature, they also become responsible, they become witnesses, they cannot remain silent anymore. Because to be silent, once you know the truth, is to become complicit. So many people would rather not know than know—and then have to do something about it.

Life becomes dangerous if you start thinking of doing something about the truth you know. I say this from my experience in Iran, but I have known it as well for many other parts of the world.

As to the other part of the question about American culture, in Iran, people might criticize America's policies, but they're in love with American culture. They know America through its culture.

I mentioned in *Republic of Imagination* that before I came to America, I knew America through its imaginary landscape. And not just me. During my teaching in Iran, for example, the head of the Islamic Students Association, one of the most powerful organizations in the universities, fell in love with America because of its films. He would smuggle in films and bring them to me and tell me to watch them.

I had one girl who was very orthodox Muslim, and I had assigned *Wuthering Heights* to her class. At the beginning of the term she came to me and said, "I object to you teaching this book. It's about adultery." At the end of the semester, she shamefacedly came to me and said, "You know, all I do in the dorm is talk about Katherine and Heathcliff. And they make fun of me. Do you have more books for me to read like that?"

You know, that is how we change people, through appealing to their hearts and minds. Yes, they fell in love with Hemingway and Ellison.

And it breaks my heart to see how America's culture is celebrated in other parts of the world, especially in the oppressed parts of the world, and it is not celebrated as much within the country itself.

CYNTHIA: This idea of stories has been recognized in politics before. President Ronald Reagan was famous for telling stories as a way to illustrate a point. The great diplomat George Shultz, who died recently at the age of one hundred, recalled Reagan suggesting that Shultz add a story to a passage in a speech because a story "will engage your readers, and that way you'll appeal not only to their minds but to their emotions."[2] Reagan understood that telling a story helps make your case in a way that no abstraction can. A story builds an emotional bond, and emotional bonds build trust.

AZAR: You mentioned Reagan's appreciation of stories, I think I will make my point through a story, one that we all know, Scheherazade of the 1,001 nights. Now, if you remember, the story was based on the fact that the king finds out that his queen has betrayed him and committed adultery, so he becomes very angry. Before giving her any chance to explain herself or have a trial, he kills her. And from then on, he generalizes that all women will betray him. Every night he would sleep with a virgin, and in the morning before she could do anything to betray him, the king would kill her.

Scheherazade, who is the vizier's daughter and is exempt from becoming a bride, nonetheless asks her father to make her marry the king. The storyteller informs us that Scheherazade was very wise, well-read, and more preoccupied with her intellectual accomplishment than her beauty. At night, when they are in the bedroom, she asks the king's permission to tell a story to her sister before she is killed. The king allows her, so she tells the story. But when the dawn comes, Scheherazade leaves the story unfinished. So the king, who wants to know what happens next, grants her another night, and this goes on for 1,001 nights until the king is cured and forgives everyone.

The kernel of this story is that stories are for our survival because at the heart of the story is curiosity. People who are not curious about others are people who only care about themselves. And we see this so much today. We see it in politics, where four hundred thousand people could die of a pandemic and a former president would not care. Sometimes this happens even in academia, when we are not curious about people we disagree with.

Now fiction is curious about everyone, including the enemy. Because if you want to win the war, you need to know the enemy. Scheherazade needs to know how she can change the king. And the general in the war needs to know how the generals on the other side think. So the whole idea of story is based on curiosity.

Once you are curious about other people, once you come out of yourself and discover others, you discover two things. One is that you can celebrate the difference. It is so much fun to know someone who doesn't see exactly the same way as you see. And the second thing is empathy. The king now puts himself in the mind of a woman, or in the mind of a queen he killed. And maybe he finds out that not all women are betrayers, and not all kings are good kings.

So it is curiosity and empathy that is at the heart of every story. And I think that The Lab has adapted the story of Jan Karski to bring out our sense of curiosity and our empathy. And that is the most humane thing one can do. I am reminded of Nabokov's saying that "curiosity is insubordination in its purest form!"[3] Because it makes you question and doubt and leave behind your assumptions and prejudices.

CYNTHIA: It's extraordinary because you have actually captured in a broader context one of our most timely projects—The Lab's In Your Shoes project, based on a deep listening methodology developed by The Lab founding co-director and director of *Remember This*, Derek Goldman. The In Your Shoes course involves Georgetown students encountering and getting to know students at Patrick Henry College, a conservative Christian college in Virginia, through the methodology of "performing one another." Participants interview each other and quite literally put themselves in someone else's shoes.

AZAR: That does exactly the opposite of what is being done right now, as so many people do not listen to the other side. In fact, they very proudly acknowledge that they do not listen.

Your program goes exactly in the opposite direction, which is the direction of fiction—namely, that before judgment, you need understanding. And this is what knowledge is all about. Whether it is scientific or literary or artistic, knowledge is based on you being curious and investigating the other and not looking for any rewards but looking for meaning, connection, and knowing the other.

CYNTHIA: A central theme throughout *Remember This: The Lesson of Jan Karski* is this question: "What does it mean to know?" The play begins with David Strathairn saying, "We see what goes on in the world." But what do we do with that knowledge? How do creative artists address that question, "What does it mean to know?"

AZAR: One of the problems I discovered when I returned to America in 1997 was evasion, evasion of pain, and our desire for constant entertainment. I mean, we turned politics into a spectacle, and everything else is also entertainment: there is a desire for intellectual comfort and complacency.

James Baldwin addresses this question of our not wanting to know: "There is something monstrous about never having been hurt . . . never having lost anything, never having gained anything, because life is beautiful . . . America is something like that. The failure on our part to accept the reality of pain, of anguish, of ambiguity of death, has turned us into a very peculiar, and sometimes monstrous people."[4] In another place, he talks about how we keep our hatred because we're trying to evade pain. We don't want to face pain.

What you were saying about Jan Karski and his fundamental question—"What does it mean to know?"—you can see it on a different level on a smaller scale right now in our political scene, with the Republican Party. But there are those few, very few, who know the risks of seeing and having to do something about what they see. And then there are quite a large number of those who choose not to know and not to see.

CYNTHIA: I'm really curious to hear you talk more about Baldwin and what Baldwin can mean for us now.

AZAR: Baldwin talked about how for a long time he hated the English language, and he didn't know what to do with it until he decided that he would take the best from what is there, and which is not his legacy, and make it his legacy. For him, literature was universal, he was not afraid of taking from others: he loved Henry James, Fyodor Dostoevsky, William Shakespeare, and the Bible, but he also brought into his writing his own unique experience, the Negro spirituals, the rhymes and rhythms of African American lives and culture. Therefore, he created a new world that had universal resonances.

And that is how I feel about literature, that those of us who are genuinely committed to works of imagination are what I call intimate strangers—we might not have ever met, but because of the passion we share, we are also intimate.

There are no boundaries of race, nationality, ethnicity, gender, language; we are all in this Republic (of Imagination). That gives me hope because no matter where I go in the world, there will be people who belong to this republic, which no one can take away from me. That is how I, a woman from Iran, can feel that James Baldwin, a black American, or Jan Karski, a Polish resistance fighter, is my kith and kin, my closest relative.

Another thing about Baldwin was that he did not belong to any one group or organization. He always had that independence of mind. And he said about himself, I am a witness, not a representative. So, as witness, he was what you mentioned about Jan Karski, that witness to the truth who must speak up.

Witnesses like Karski and Baldwin by nature cannot remain silent. They have to tell the truth not because they are politicized, not because they belong to a political party or have a political agenda, but because it's the right thing to do.

Notes

1. Bryan Boyd, *Vladimir Nabokov: The American Years* (Princeton, NJ: Princeton University Press, 1990), 91.

2. Quoted in George P. Shultz, "The Ten Most Important Things I've Learned about Trust over My 100 Years," *Washington Post*, December 11, 2020.

3. Vladimir Nabokov, *Bend Sinister* (New York: Knopf, 1990), 46.

4. James Baldwin, *The Cross of Redemption: Uncollected Writings* (New York: Vintage 2010), 79.

AFTERWORD

Leo J. O'Donovan, SJ

As it was an honor and a blessing to have known Jan Karski, so too is it a blessed honor, at the end of this volume celebrating and dramatizing Jan's life, to trace my own steps on the way to what is offered here.

My first experience of the play was at a workshop performance at a little place on Manhattan's Theater Row, when David Strathairn's appearance as Jan Karski stunned me not so much with his physical as much as his spiritual evocation of Jan. Yes, David is almost as lean as Jan was. But it was the dignity, the humble authority, the sense of purpose, the eyes that saw so far that brought me to tears. David was supported by young actors playing various parts (especially students), scripts in hand. At the end I could not for a while leave my seat, and when I then went to congratulate David on his performance, I found that I could not for a while speak.

The next iteration was at the Museum of Jewish Heritage in downtown Manhattan, now with a somewhat older supporting cast but with David evoking Karski's spirit even more tellingly. At a panel discussion afterward, I again found it at first hard to speak. So, too, at the centennial celebration of Georgetown's School of Foreign Service in November 2019, at a performance of the play in Gaston Hall, with David now alone on a stage bare but for a table and chair and clearly giving a definitive performance, I struggled to contain tears and say something, at the panel that followed, worthy of our beloved actor's incarnation of a man worthy of veneration as a saint.

But who would expect to be able to speak any but Jan's words, he who kept silent for so many years and only painfully realized that he must bear witness? Who dares speak, except in hushed, afflicted tones of the horror to which he witnessed? But now we have a dramatic record of that witness to wring our hearts and offer them the courage to speak the truth as well.

The following text was the homily for the Funeral Mass for Jan Karski at the Cathedral of St. Matthew the Apostle in Washington, DC, on July 18, 2000. The readings for the Mass were Wisdom 3:1–9, Romans 5:5–11, and Mark 15:33–39.

Your Excellencies, beloved friends and faculty, colleagues of Dr. Karski, mourning visitors from Poland, dear Jewish friends:

It was the eyes that you remembered, the searching, pale, blue Polish eyes that always saw beyond, and understood, and remembered.

The man came from another place and time, one felt, a place of dignity and integrity, a time of courage and commitment, a community of just men and women who cared for each other deeply and equally. But he seemed to come from a place of peace only because first, and profoundly, he had passed through such suffering. "I saw terrible things," he would simply, searingly say.

The handsome, commanding face of the aristocratic young diplomat aged—savage Nazi torture more than hastened the process. The tall, lean frame grew bent and fragile. But the piercing eyes became somehow resolute, unforgettable, windows to the witness of a century's gaping horror and faint hope, its deepest abysses and its glimmer of possible salvation.

Born on the twenty-fourth of April 1914 as the youngest of eight children of the Kozielewski family in the industrial city of Łódź (Karski was, of course, his later name as a secret agent),

Jan showed great talent at the Jesuit school he attended, became a young man of ardent faith, and appeared to have a distinguished career before him when, on completing two master's degrees at the Jan Kazimierz University in Lwów, he entered the Polish diplomatic service. But then the great crevice of the twentieth century engulfed him, as we know now, though for decades he sought through silence to escape the scenes of suffering he had seen.

After enlisting in the army in 1939, he was captured by Soviet troops but then escaped from their detention camp. He joined the Polish Underground and became one of its finest couriers but was captured again in 1940, this time by the Gestapo, and even tried to kill himself by slashing his wrists so as to avoid divulging secret information. Amazingly, he was rescued from the hospital and returned to his underground work. This led to his mission in 1942 to bring news of the Polish situation to the West. Preparing for that, Jan managed to visit the Ghetto of Warsaw and a death camp in Izbica Lubelska so that he could assure London and Washington that Hitler's threatened extermination of the Jews was the hideous truth.

But neither Anthony Eden nor Franklin Roosevelt nor Felix Frankfurter in 1943 could really believe the young witness to unspeakable horror, and it was only on the publication of his memoir *Story of a Secret State* in 1944 that Karski's heroism in revealing the Holocaust began to be recognized.

Years later Jan would say of this time:

The Lord assigned me a role to speak and write during the war, when—as it seemed to me—it might help. It did not . . .

Then I became a Jew. Like the family of my wife [in 1965 Jan had married the dancer and choreographer Pola Nirenska]—all of them perished in the ghettos, in the concentration camps, in the gas chambers—so all murdered Jews became my family.

But I am a Christian Jew. I am a practicing Catholic . . . My faith tells me the second Original Sin has been committed by humanity: through commission, or omission, or self-imposed ignorance, or insensitivity, or self-interest, or hypocrisy, or heartless rationalization.

This sin will haunt humanity to the end of time.

"It does haunt me," he said. "And I want it to be so."[1]

This is where, for the most part, the popular account of Jan Karski's life generally ends. A man who had seen unspeakable suffering and announced it to the world, in 1981, expressed his profound resignation. (One year later, nevertheless, he was recognized by the Israeli government as one of the "Righteous Among the Nations.")

There were, however, other things that Jan Karski saw, and if today we are adequately to remember this just man (Wisd. 3:1) in whose heart the Spirit of God dwelt (Rom. 5:5), they must be mentioned.

And they were these: First, this country. And second, his university. And third, the judgment to come.

"This blessed land," he often called America, and in my hearing at no time more eloquently than this past May 23 when he returned from Poland at four o'clock in the morning, so as to attend a dinner given by the Anti-Defamation League and honoring Cardinal Hickey, who was to be presented the Jan Karski Award. Jan spoke first, and memorably, invoking for a mesmerized audience what a "blessed land" this was. He was puzzled by the United States, however. He always remained very European in dress and manner. But he had a clear passion for American democracy, for American opportunity, for American equality. After the war, he had not been able to allow himself to return to a communist Poland and in 1954 became a naturalized American citizen. He loved his native land, of course, and remained always a Polish hero. But he spoke so eloquently, urging his hearers always "not to forget, dear friends, this blessed land."

He came also to see every part of his university. In 1943, during his first visit to inform the American government of the Holocaust, he had met Father Edmund Walsh, the founder and then regent of the School of Foreign Service at Georgetown University. In 1949 he returned to visit Father Walsh and ask for his advice. Father Walsh, whom Jan admired as a Renaissance prince capable of being quite imperious, told him that even though he was thirty-five and had two advanced degrees, he must go back to school and begin a full doctoral program. Then, on the very evening that he received his PhD, there was a telegram waiting from Father Walsh to invite him to become a member of the Georgetown faculty.

His classes were enormously popular and enormously effective. He specialized in the theory of communism and comparative politics and in 1985 published his major work, *The Great Powers and Poland, 1919–1945: From Versailles to Yalta*. But it was the students and his colleagues of whom he was proudest. He supported the new young dean, Peter Krogh, steadily and readily through all Peter's remarkable leadership. He was proud when so distinguished a faculty member as Madeleine Korbel Albright was chosen to fill his position when he retired. And there are other things as well from his tenure at Georgetown that we should remember, certainly his deep commitment to alleviating poverty—and his wonderful, wry sense of humor.

Jan Karski died at Georgetown University Hospital on the thirteenth of July in the year 2000, on the Hilltop, which had been his academic home for over half a century. There he kept silent about what he had seen, then spoke of it for humanity's sake. At war's end, he said, "I hated humanity." But gradually, for humanity's sake, he spoke. National audiences, but students especially, listened. At Georgetown he saw generations of students pass through his classes and knew, in his keen, modest way, how they marveled at his teaching, his political passion, his mysterious person.

But Jan Karski saw more: he had seen the cross of Christ at the gulf of the century, he had heard the cry of abandonment from millions of brothers and sisters of Jesus of Nazareth. He knew he was preparing to see still more—his God. He said some years ago:

I don't show it, but I am a religious man. I know God gives us not collective but individual conscience. It is this beautiful part of man. He has a choice. He is free to follow evil; he is free to choose right. Everyone is responsible to his Creator individually.

There will come a moment when I will be called. This will be the last judgment. God will say to me: "Karski, I gave you your soul. Your body died. Your soul is mine. I gave it to you. What did you do with your soul?"

And I will have to answer. I want to make heaven. I want to make salvation.

I am old and no longer strong. I don't need courage anymore. So, I teach compassion.[2]

And so, in the final years of his retirement, he did indeed continue to teach compassion. And every Sunday he went to St. Ann's to receive communion, even after the terrible affliction of his wife's death in 1992. And now he has died and left us.

Some months ago, though, he wrote and sent me a very generous gift asking that I do with it whatever I choose. We now have a scholarship in honor of Pola, his wife. And the Stations of the Cross in Dahlgren Chapel are now illuminated through Jan's gift. As with Mark's Gospel (Mark 15:33–16:8), the Stations of the Cross end at the tomb, not yet offering a vision of the risen Christ. But that is whom Jan surely sees now—Christ and his Father. Again, he keeps silence about what he sees. But surely in our prayer he will tell us of his judgment. And one day he will tell us in his own words how he made salvation.

Notes

1. Stefan Korboński, *The Jews and the Poles in World War II* (New York: Hippocrene, 1989), 103.

2. *Washingtonian* 23 (1988): 67.

I don't need courage anymore. So, I teach compassion.

ACKNOWLEDGMENTS

David Strathairn is the Willie Mays of collaborators—a five-tool player who catches everything. His love for the game is contagious, his grace and humility are unparalleled, and his skill is breathtaking. Thank you for your commitment, your friendship, and your heart.

Three people were the architects of the project's expansion into the medium of film. Producer Eva Anisko made it all happen through sheer willpower, vision, and positive spirit. She assembled an extraordinary film and postproduction team who worked tirelessly and safely to create this film during the COVID-19 pandemic. Co-director and director of photography Jeff Hutchens brought a virtuosic cinematic vision to every stage of production as well as an assiduous attention to detail. He erased every fly in the ointment. Co-producer Alexander Hyde is a wizard who can find a sweater vest anywhere.

Michael Donnay has been more than an unflappably professional stage and production manager for this project—he has been part dramaturg, part script supervisor, and all-around theater-maker.

The creative team for our theatrical production—movement director Emma Jaster, set designer Misha Kachman, composer and sound designer Roc Lee, lighting designer Alberto Segarra, and costume designer Ivania Stack—created the elegant and visceral world of the play, and they brought joy, ingenuity, and geography lessons to the rehearsal space.

The co-founder of The Laboratory for Global Performance and Politics, Ambassador Cynthia Schneider, has blessed this project with her wisdom, experience, and passion in myriad ways. Dean Joel Hellman embraced The Lab's mission and vision as part of the Walsh School of Foreign Service and believed in it enough to feature it as a centerpiece of the school's centennial in Georgetown's Gaston Hall as well as in our subsequent journey to London in conjunction with International Holocaust Remembrance Day and the seventy-fifth anniversary of the liberation of Auschwitz. Incalculable thanks to our amazing team at The Lab, including Madeleine Kelley, who gamely assisted in this editing process; Erin Donohue; Mélisande Short-Colomb; Alyssa Kardos; and Sarah Ginnetti; and, in earlier stages of the project, Jojo Ruf and Rob Jansen.

The educational platform Bearing Witness: The Legacy of Jan Karski Today owes its depth of pedagogy to its co-creator, our brilliant Lab colleague Ijeoma Njaka. We are grateful to Randy Bass for his vision and invaluable support, and for his invitation for us to develop the course as part of the Just Communities Initiative. Our wonderful collaborators Alexander Hage and Paolo Matchett helped build the remarkable course website. Thank you to the students who first piloted the course in the challenging fall of 2020—Julia Lo Casio, Domenic Desantes, Christian Ficca, Sarah Green, Jessica Hornick, Leigh Meyer, Jesse Ryno, Amina Sadural, and Emily Sweeney. Each of you brought poignant personal history and eloquent perspective to the story of Jan Karski and its application today. We learned so much from you and will continue to do so.

Thank you to individual producing partners, collaborators, and advocates throughout these stages, including Andrzej Rojek, Ewa Junczyk-Ziomecka, and Bozena Zaremba at the Jan Karski Educational Foundation, who work tirelessly to advance Karski's story, as well as Carole Zawatsky, Dan Logan, Scott Miller, Rachel Chanoff, Carol Avery, Erica Zielinski, Debbie Bisno, Simon Godwin, Chris Jennings, Robert Billingsley, Michal Mrozek, Wanda Urbanska, Michael Abramowitz, Paul Tagliabue, Chan Tagliabue, Miranda

Dunbar-Johnson, Sarah von Thun-Hohenstein, David Marwell, Bruce Ratner, the Museum of Jewish Heritage in New York, Tomasz Karolak, Przemyslaw Krych, Scott Fleming, Susan Ellicott, Laura Apelbaum, Andrew Ammerman, Emily Mann, Ari Roth, Laley Lippard, Roberta Pereira, Dan Brumberg, Joseph Megel, Tom Banchoff, Daniel Phoenix Singh, and Georgetown University president, John J. DeGioia.

The Department of Performing Arts at Georgetown has been this project's longtime partner. Thank you to our friends and colleagues there, especially Maya Roth, Soyica Colbert, Natsu Onoda Power, Christine Evans, and Toby Clark for his mastery of all things Zoom.

Six years of development require a lot of help and gratitude. Thank you to the spaces that have been home to the development of this play, including Georgetown University, Teatr IMKA, Theater Row, the Museum of Jewish Heritage, Shakespeare Theatre Company, McCarter Theatre Center, and Queen Mary University. Thank you to all our producing partners including THE OFFICE performing arts + film, the Jan Karski Educational Foundation, Georgetown University's School of Foreign Service, Georgetown University's Department of Performing Arts, the POLIN Museum of the History of Polish Jews, the National Academy of Theatre Arts in Kraków, the United States Holocaust Memorial Museum, and Human Rights Watch.

Thank you to the ensembles of students and crew members who worked on staged readings of the play in its developmental stages. They include:

At Georgetown—Maria Edmundson, Peter Fanone, Greg Keiser, Walter Kelly, Ben Prout, Shannon Walsh, and Addison Williams.

In Warsaw—Anna Antoniewicz, Sebastian Grygo, Tomas Kolarik, Maciej Kulig, Mateusz Malecki, Monika Mazur, Piotr Nerlewski, Addison Williams, Tomasz Wlosok, Katarzyna Zagorska, and Małgorzata Zielińska.

Thank you to the ensembles of professional actors and crew members who worked on staged readings. Special thanks to the indefatigable Stephanie Klapper, casting director extraordinaire. The ensembles include:

At Theater Row, New York City—Ari Brand, Eric Berryman, Molly Camp, Ethan Dubin, Laura C. Harris, Joe Isenberg, Katya Stepanov, and Harlan Work.

At the Museum of Jewish Heritage, New York City—Jo Farrow, Kate Freer, Jen Schriever, Kersti Bryan, Connie Castanzo, Nicholas Carrierre, Joshua Landay, Mariko Parker, P. J. Sosko, and Robbie Tan.

Thank you to the film crew of *Remember This*—Scott Buckler, Filipp Penson, Melissa Gagliardi, T. J. Alston, Pete Milmoe, Keagan Fuller, Bill Hilferty, Corey Jacobs, Bryan Landes, Aaron Chandler, Walid Alhamdy, Timothy Daly, and Christian Sylvester.

Thank you to the postproduction film team of *Remember This*— Brandon Bray, Beth Levison, Alistair Mackay, Ric Schnupp, Roland Vajs, Nuno Bento, Joao Galvao, Jevon Johnson, Phil Fuller, Ashley Foy, Jay Rubin, Paul Bronkar, Tom Younghans, George Bunce, Keith Jenson, Spyros Katsihtis, Sean Perry, Tom Younghans, Andrew McKay, Pete Olshansky, John Albrecht, and Steven LaMorte.

Many lent their work, time, and stories to us over the course of this project. Students, friends, and admirers of Jan Karski are the reason his legacy lives on, people like Speaker Nancy Pelosi, Paul Pelosi, Christiane Amanpour, Father Patrick Desbois, Father Dennis McManus, Rabbi Rachel Gartner, Razia Iqbal, Penny Green, E. Thomas Wood, Slawomir Grünberg, and Laura Schandelmeier. Thank you for your commitment to Karski and to the continued hard work of telling his story.

Al Bertrand, Elizabeth Crowley Webber, Caroline Crossman, and the team at Georgetown University Press, and Patricia Bower of Diligent Editorial, made this publication happen at an impossible pace. Thank you to all of the volume's distinguished contributors—Secretary Madeleine Albright, Ambassador Stuart Eizenstat, Aminatta Forna, Azar Nafisi, Father Leo O'Donovan, Ambassador Samantha Power, Ambassador Cynthia Schneider, Timothy Snyder, and Deborah Tannen—who so potently and poignantly carry Jan Karski's legacy into today's world. We are honored to be in your company.

Thank you to our friends and family who bring laughs, love, and beer, Polish vodka, or spiked kombucha, depending on the author. Special and infinite gratitude to Caroline, Emily, Chas, and Oliver, who make our lives and hearts full, as well as Margery and Peter Arnold, Maynard and Suzanne Goldman, and Clark and Ann Young.

This work honors the spirits of Jan Karski, Pola Nirenska, and Szmul Zygielbojm, and all those who continue to bear witness.

REFERENCES

Books

Baldwin, James. *The Cross of Redemption: Uncollected Writings*. New York: Vintage, 2010.

Boyd, Bryan. *Vladimir Nabokov: The American Years*. Princeton, NJ: Princeton University Press, 1990.

Feldman, Lily Gardner. *The Special Relationship between West Germany and Israel*. London: George Allen & Unwin, 1984.

Karski, Jan. *Story of a Secret State: My Report to the World*. Washington, DC: Georgetown University Press, 2014.

Korboński, Stefan. *The Jews and the Poles in World War II*. New York: Hippocrene, 1989.

Lacquer, Walter. *The Terrible Secret: Suppression of the Truth about Hitler's "Final Solution."* New York: Penguin, 1982.

Nabokov, Vladimir. *Bend Sinister*. New York: Knopf, 1990.

Snyder, Timothy. *Bloodlands: Europe between Hitler and Stalin*. New York: Basic Books, 2012.

———. *Black Earth: The Holocaust as History and Warning*. New York: Random House, 2015.

Newspaper Articles

Kaufman, Michael T. "Jan Karski Dies at 86; Warned West about Holocaust." *New York Times*, July 15, 2000. https://www.nytimes.com/2000/07/15/world/jan-karski-dies-at-86-warned-west-about-holocaust.html.

Koestler, Arthur. "The Nightmare That Is a Reality." *New York Times*, January 9, 1944.

Shultz, George P. "The Ten Most Important Things I've Learned about Trust over My 100 Years." *Washington Post*, December 11, 2020. https://www.washingtonpost.com/opinions/2020/12/11/10-most-important-things-ive-learned-about-trust-over-my-100-years.

Vulliamy, Ed. "Revealer of Holocaust Secret Dies." *Guardian*, July 15, 2000. https://www.theguardian.com/world/2000/jul/16/edvulliamy.theobserver.

US and UK Government Documents

385 Parl. Deb. H.C. (5th ser.) (1942) cols. 2082–87. https://api.parliament.uk/historic-hansard/commons/1942/dec/17/united-nations-declaration.

Albert A. Hutler Collection. "Articles and U.S. military records relating to displaced persons in postwar Europe." US Holocaust Memorial Museum, Washington, DC.

Web Materials

Conference on Jewish Material Claims Against Germany. "U.S. Millennial Holocaust Knowledge and Awareness Survey." Accessed on March 6, 2021. http://www.claimscon.org/millennial-study/.

FURTHER READING

Resources and Recommended Works

The following works have been critical sources in the creation of this play:

Karski, Jan. "Holocaust Rescuer and Aid Provider Jan Karski Testimony."
    Interview by Renee Firestone. USC Shoah Foundation. March 10, 1995.
———. "Jan Karski." Interview by Claude Lanzmann. Claude Lanzmann
    Shoah Collection. United States Holocaust Memorial Museum, Wash-
    ington, DC. October 1978.
———. *Story of a Secret State: My Report to the World.* Washington, DC:
    Georgetown University Press, 2014.
———. "Oral History with Jan Karski." Interview by Gay Block and Malka
    Drucker. United States Holocaust Memorial Museum, Washington, DC.
    February 22, 1988.
Lanzmann, Claude, dir. *Shoah.* 1985; New York: Criterion Collection,
    2013. DVD.
Wood, E. Thomas, and Stanisław M. Jankowski. *Karski: How One Man Tried
    to Stop the Holocaust.* New York: John Wiley, 1994.

Additional Recommended Works

Foer, Jonathan Safran. *We Are the Weather: Saving the Planet Begins at
    Breakfast.* New York: Farrar, Straus and Giroux, 2019.

Grünberg, Sławomir, dir. *Karski and the Lords of Humanity*. San Francisco: Kanopy Streaming, 2015.

Haenel, Yannick. *The Messenger*. Translated by Ian Monk. New York: Counterpoint, 2012.

Harrison, Carol. *Jan Karski: Photographs*. [McLean, Virginia?]: Carol Harrison Fine Art Photography, 2013.

Jan Karski Educational Foundation. jankarski.net.

Karski, Jan, *The Great Powers and Poland: From Versailles to Yalta*. Lanham, MD: Rowman & Littlefield, 2014. First published in 1985 by University Press of American (Lanham).

Lanzmann, Claude, dir. *The Karski Report*. France, 2010.

Medoff, Rafael. *Karski's Mission: To Stop the Holocaust*. Washington, DC: Jan Karski Educational Foundation, 2015.

Pola Nirenska collection. Library of Congress, Washington, DC. https://www.loc.gov/item/2003682047/.

CONTRIBUTORS

MADELEINE ALBRIGHT served as the sixty-fourth secretary of state of the United States. In 1997 she was named the first female secretary of state and became, at that time, the highest-ranking woman in the history of the US government. From 1993 to 1997 Dr. Albright served as the US permanent representative to the United Nations. She is a professor at the Georgetown University School of Foreign Service. Dr. Albright is chair of Albright Stonebridge Group and chair of Albright Capital Management LLC. She also chairs the National Democratic Institute. In 2012 she was chosen by President Barack Obama to receive the Presidential Medal of Freedom. Dr. Albright is a seven-time *New York Times* best-selling author.

EVA ANISKO is an award-winning producer with experience spearheading social-issue documentaries, news and public affairs television series, and multiplatform programming, including PBS series: *Blueprint America*, Emmy Award–winning *Exposé: America's Investigative Reports*, and the sustainable design series *Design: e2*, narrated by Brad Pitt. In addition to producing the film *Remember This*, Eva produced the Emmy Award-winning feature documentary, *The Armor of Light* (dir. Abigail Disney). Other films include: *Buffalo Returns* (dir. Gini Reticker); *In the Footsteps of Marco Polo*;

Beyond the Motor City; and *A Place in Time* (dir. Angelina Jolie). Eva received her bachelor of arts degree from Georgetown University and master of education from Harvard University.

STUART EIZENSTAT is a senior counsel of Covington & Burling LLP in its international practice. During a decade and a half of public service, Ambassador Eizenstat has held a number of key senior positions, including chief White House domestic policy advisor to President Jimmy Carter (1977–81), US ambassador to the European Union, undersecretary of commerce, undersecretary of state, and deputy secretary of the Treasury in the Clinton administration (1993–2001). He also served as a member of the White House staff for President Lyndon Johnson (1967–68). In addition, during the Clinton administration, he served as special representative of the president and secretary of state on Holocaust-era issues. During the Obama administration he served as special advisor on Holocaust-era issues to secretaries of state Hillary Clinton and John Kerry (2009–17). During the Trump administration he was appointed as expert advisor to the State Department on Holocaust-era issues, a position he continues to hold in the Biden administration (2018–21). He is the author of the books *Imperfect Justice: Looted Assets, Slave Labor, and the Unfinished Business of World War II* and *President Carter: The White House Years.*

AMINATTA FORNA is a novelist, memoirist, and essayist. Her novels are *Happiness, The Hired Man, The Memory of Love*, and *Ancestor Stones*. In 2002 she published a memoir of her dissident father and Sierra Leone, *The Devil That Danced on the Water. The Window Seat*, an essay collection, was published by Grove Press in 2021. She received the Windham–Campbell Prize from Yale University and the Commonwealth Writers' Prize. Forna was made an OBE in the Queen's 2017 New Year's Honours list. Aminatta Forna is Lannan Chair of Poets and director of the Lannan Center for Poetics and Social Practice at Georgetown University.

DEREK GOLDMAN, co-author and stage director of *Remember This: The Lesson of Jan Karski*, is chair of Georgetown University's Department of Performing Arts and director of the Theater & Performance Studies Program as well as co-founding director of The Laboratory for Global Performance and Politics. He is an award-winning stage director, playwright, scholar, producer, and developer of new work, whose work has been seen around the country, off-Broadway, and internationally. He is the author of more than thirty professionally produced plays and adaptations, and he has directed more than one hundred productions. He holds a PhD in performance studies from Northwestern University, and he received the President's Award for Distinguished Scholar-Teachers at Georgetown.

JEFF HUTCHENS, co-director and director of photography for *Remember This*, is a cinematographer who grew up across the United States, China, South Africa, and the Philippines. After ten years on the road as an award-winning magazine photojournalist (*Time*, *New York Times Magazine*, *National Geographic*), Jeff switched mediums and brought his innovative visual aesthetic into filmmaking. He has worked in more than sixty countries, exploring social and cultural issues around the world with a long-form blend of intimate naturalism and surrealist noir. His cinematography credits include numerous feature documentaries and documentary series for Showtime, HBO, and Netflix. He is based in Washington, DC.

ALEXANDER HYDE co-produced the film adaptation of *Remember This*. Originally from the United Kingdom, he has spent the past eight years producing award-winning films that document the American experience, covering everything from music legends Bruce Springsteen and Johnny Cash to pressing social issues including the Iraq War protests and wealth inequality. His forthcoming directorial debut, *The Interruption*, follows a self-help guru preaching American individualism in mainland China.

AZAR NAFISI is best known as the author of the national best seller *Reading Lolita in Tehran: A Memoir in Books*, which has spent over 117 weeks on the *New York Times* best-seller list. She has published a children's book (with illustrator Sophie Benini Pietromarchi) *BiBi and the Green Voice*. She is also the author of a memoir about her mother titled *Things I've Been Silent About: Memories of a Prodigal Daughter*. Additionally, she wrote *The Republic of Imagination: America in Three Books*. Azar Nafisi's book on Vladimir Nabokov, *That Other World*, was published by Yale University Press in June 2019. She is currently exploring the power of literature in traumatic times in her forthcoming book *Read Dangerously: The Subversive Power of Literature in Troubled Times* (HarperCollins/Dey Street Books, 2022).

LEO J. O'DONOVAN, SJ, served as president of the Catholic Theological Society of America from 1981 to 1982 and in 1989 was elected the forty-seventh president of Georgetown University, serving in that capacity until 2001. A systematic theologian who also writes art criticism, he is a professor of theology at Georgetown and currently resides in New York City, where he writes, lectures, and has been a visiting professor at Fordham University, Union Theological Seminary, and General Theological Seminary. In January 2016 he was appointed director of mission for the Jesuit Refugee Service/USA in Washington, DC. In 2018, with Scott Rose as co-editor, he published *Blessed Are the Refugees: Beatitudes of Immigrant Children*, with a foreword by Joe Biden. In 2021 he delivered the invocation at the inauguration of President Biden.

SAMANTHA POWER is the administrator of the US Agency for International Development. She previously served from 2013 to 2017 as the US ambassador to the United Nations and from 2009 to 2013 on the National Security Council as special assistant to the president for multilateral affairs and human rights. Power began her career as a journalist and was the founding executive director of the Carr Center for Human Rights Policy at Harvard Kennedy

School. Power is the author of *"A Problem from Hell": America and the Age of Genocide,* which won the Pulitzer Prize in 2003, *Chasing the Flame: One Man's Fight to Save the World* (2008), and *The Education of an Idealist: A Memoir* (2019).

CYNTHIA SCHNEIDER, PhD, Distinguished Professor in the Practice of Diplomacy at Georgetown University, teaches, publishes, and organizes initiatives in diplomacy and culture. She co-directs The Laboratory for Global Performance and Politics at Georgetown as well as the Los Angeles–based MOST Resource (Muslims on Screen and Television) and the Mali-based Timbuktu Renaissance. She publishes and speaks on topics related to arts, culture, and media and international affairs. Professor Schneider was a member of Georgetown's art history faculty from 1984 to 2005 and published on Rembrandt and seventeenth-century Dutch art. From 1998 to 2001 she served as US ambassador to the Netherlands and led initiatives in cultural diplomacy, biotechnology, cyber security, and military affairs. Professor Schneider earned a BA and PhD from Harvard University.

TIMOTHY SNYDER is the Richard C. Levin Professor of History at Yale University and a permanent fellow at the Institute for Human Sciences in Vienna. He is perhaps best known for his political pamphlets *Our Malady* and *On Tyranny* and for his public activism for the rule of law and democracy. His work has been translated into more than forty languages, and his words have been quoted in protests and demonstrations around the world. His major scholarly works include *Nationalism, Marxism, and Modern Central Europe: A Biography of Kazimierz Kelles-Krauz, 1872–1905* (1998); *The Reconstruction of Nations: Poland, Ukraine, Lithuania, Belarus, 1569–1999* (2003); *Sketches from a Secret War: A Polish Artist's Mission to Liberate Soviet Ukraine* (2005); *The Red Prince: The Secret Lives of a Habsburg Archduke* (2008); *Bloodlands: Europe between Hitler and Stalin* (2010), *Thinking the Twentieth Century* (with Tony Judt, 2012); *Black Earth: The Holocaust as History and*

Warning (2015); *On Tyranny: Twenty Lessons from the Twentieth Century* (2017); and *The Road to Unfreedom: Russia, Europe, America* (2018).

DAVID STRATHAIRN, in collaboration with Derek Goldman and Clark Young, joined with The Laboratory for Global Performance and Politics to create *Remember This: The Lesson of Jan Karski*. Other projects of which Strathairn is most proud of being a part include the Theatre of War Productions, community-specific theater-based projects that address vital public health and social issues; George Clooney's film *Good Night and Good Luck*; Steven Spielberg's *Lincoln*; Chloé Zhao's *Nomadland*; John Sayles's films *Matewan, Eight Men Out*, and *City of Hope*; Doug Magee's *Beyond the Call*; and the plays *Scorched* by Wajdi Mouawad and *Underneath the Lintel* by Glenn Berger at the American Conservatory Theater in San Francisco.

DEBORAH TANNEN is a university professor at Georgetown University. Among her twenty-six books, *You Just Don't Understand: Women and Men in Conversation* was on the *New York Times* bestseller list for nearly four years, was number 1 for eight months, and is translated into thirty-one languages. Her books *You Were Always Mom's Favorite!* and *You're Wearing THAT?* were also *New York Times* best sellers. Her most recent is the memoir *Finding My Father: His Century-Long Journey from World War I Warsaw and My Quest to Follow*. She has also published poems, short stories, and personal essays. Her play *An Act of Devotion* is included in *The Best American Short Plays 1993–1994*.

CLARK YOUNG is a writer and teacher based in Brooklyn and originally from Portland, Maine. Alongside Derek Goldman and David Strathairn, he co-created every iteration of *Remember This: The Lesson of Jan Karski*. A Georgetown graduate, Clark went on to gain his master's degree in performance studies at New York

University Tisch School of the Arts. He has since taught theater at Georgetown and Bronx Lighthouse College Prep Academy. As an actor, he has appeared in over twenty professional productions. Clark is currently workshopping his new play, *.406 Below*, about cryonics, baseball, family, and immortality.